HOTSPOTS
MEX

Thomas Cook

Cancún and the Riviera Maya

Written by Jane Egginton and Iain MacIntyre
Front cover photography courtesy of Thomas Cook Tour Operations Ltd

Original design concept by Studio 183 Limited
Series design by the Bridgewater Book Company
Cover design/artwork by Lee Biggadike, Studio 183 Limited

Produced by the Bridgewater Book Company
The Old Candlemakers, West Street, Lewes, East Sussex BN7 2NZ, United Kingdom
www.bridgewaterbooks.co.uk
Project Editor: Emily Casey Bailey
Project Designer: Lisa McCormick

Published by Thomas Cook Publishing
A division of Thomas Cook Tour Operations Limited
PO Box 227, Unit 18, Coningsby Road, Peterborough PE3 8SB, United Kingdom
email: books@thomascook.com
www.thomascookpublishing.com
+ 44 (0) 1733 416477

ISBN 13: 978-1-84157-563-6
ISBN 10: 1-84157-563-1

First edition © 2006 Thomas Cook Publishing
Text © 2006 Thomas Cook Publishing
Maps © 2006 Thomas Cook Publishing
Project Editor: Diane Ashmore
Production/DTP Editor: Steven Collins

Printed and bound in Spain by Graficas Cems, Navarra, Spain

All rights reserved. No part of this publication may be reproduced, stored in a retrieval system or transmitted, in any form or by any means, electronic, mechanical, recording or otherwise, in any part of the world, without prior permission of the publisher. Requests for permission should be made to the publisher at the above address.

Although every care has been taken in compiling this publication, and the contents are believed to be correct at the time of printing, Thomas Cook Tour Operations Limited cannot accept any responsibility for errors or omission, however caused, or for changes in details given in the guidebook, or for the consequences of any reliance on the information provided. Descriptions and assessments are based on the author's views and experiences when writing and do not necessarily represent those of Thomas Cook Tour Operations Limited.

CONTENTS

SYMBOLS KEY 4

INTRODUCTION 5
Map of Mexico 6
Getting to know Cancún
 & the Riviera Maya 8
The best of Cancún &
 the Riviera Maya 13

RESORTS 15
Cancún 16
Isla Mujeres 27
Puerto Morelos 36
Playa del Carmen & Playacar.....42
Puerto Aventuras 51
Cozumel 60
Akumal 66

EXCURSIONS 73
Pre-Hispanic culture 74
 Chichén Itzá 75
 Cobá 77
 Teotihuacán 78
 Tulum 80
Jungles, rivers & wildlife 82
 Sian Ka'an Biosphere 82

Xcaret 82
Xel-Ha 85
Colonial history 86
 Mérida 86
 Valladolid 86
Air tours 88
 Panoramic flights 89
 Private charter flights 90
Mexico City 91

LIFESTYLE 95
Food & drink 96
Menu decoder 99
Shopping 101
Kids 103
Sports & activities 106
Festivals & events 108

PRACTICAL INFORMATION 113
Preparing to go 114
During your stay 118

INDEX 125

ACKNOWLEDGEMENTS 128

HOTSPOTS

SYMBOLS KEY

The following is a key to the symbols used throughout this book:

- **i** information office
- **🚌** bus stop
- **✉** post office
- **✝** church
- **🛡** police station
- **✈** airport
- **🛒** supermarket
- **✚** hospital
- **↘** tip
- **🛍** shopping
- **🍴** restaurant
- **☕** café
- **🍸** bar
- **🍲** fine dining

- **☏** telephone
- **✆** fax
- **@** email
- **w** website address
- **a** address
- **🕐** opening times
- **!** important
- **€** budget price **€€** mid-range price **€€€** most expensive
- **★** specialist interest **★★** see if passing **★★★** top attraction

INTRODUCTION
Getting to know Cancún & the Riviera Maya

UNITED S
MEXICALI
EL PASO
SAN QUINTÍN
CHIHUAHUA
Rio Bravo
Rio Grande
SANTA ROSALÍA
CIUDAD OBREGÓN
HIDALGO DEL PARRAL
LORETO
TARREÓN
SAL
LA PAZ
DURANGO
MAZATIÁN
ZACATECAS::
SA
PACIFIC OCEAN
GUADALAJARA
Teotihua
N
0
300 km
0
300 miles

CANADA
USA
MEXICO
Gulf of Mexico
CUBA
Pacific Ocean
CENTRAL AMERICA
GULF OF MEXICO
AD VICTORIA
TAMPICO
MÉRIDA
CANCÚN
CAMPECHE
SEE MAP ON PAGE 11
CARIBBEAN SEA
EXICO CITY
VILLAHERMOSA
BELIZE
TUXTLA GUTIÉRREZ
SALINA CRUZ
HONDURAS
GUATEMALA
EL SALVADOR
NICARAGUA

INTRODUCTION

INTRODUCTION

Getting to know Cancún & the Riviera Maya

Mexico conjures up images of cowboys and Indians, deserts and cacti, tequila and tropical jungle. As a holiday destination, it is exotic yet friendly, with a sunny climate and delicious food. The country has world-class beaches, a rich culture and great shopping. Well established as a tourist destination, its resorts are sophisticated, while much of the countryside is unspoilt.

Mexico is sandwiched between the southern states of the US and the Central American countries of Guatemala and Belize. It is flanked by the huge sweep of the Gulf of Mexico and the Caribbean Sea to the east and the Pacific Ocean on its western side.

Cancún and the Riviera Maya form a strip on the eastern coast of the Yucatán Peninsula – a large tongue of land on the Caribbean coast of Mexico. The area's high concentration of spectacular beaches and Mayan sites make it extremely popular. Cancún is without doubt the holiday-makers' mecca, but the long string of much smaller and quieter resorts stretching south (known as the Riviera Maya) are gaining in popularity.

Spanish is spoken throughout the country, although many people are unaware that more than 50 native Indian languages are also in use. In tourist areas, English is widely spoken, but a little Spanish goes a long way (see page 122 for some useful words and phrases).

HISTORY

This is a land rich in history, well known for its archaeological remains and its folk art. The Spanish first arrived in Mexico on Isla Mujeres in 1517 (see page 27). In the space of a few short and brutal years, the Spanish conquered the entire country, and held onto it for three centuries. As a result, 60 per cent of today's population is a mix of Spanish and Indian descent, known as *mestizo*.

◀ *Man dressed in typical costume from western Mexico*

INTRODUCTION

THE MEXICAN PEOPLE

The people of Mexico – approximately 100 million strong, with one fifth crammed in around Mexico City – are as diverse as the country's destinations, and Indians, descendants of Mexico's pre-Hispanic inhabitants, have retained much of their culture and language. Visitors will also notice that the family is very important here and mothers are greatly revered. The country is deeply religious – around 90 per cent of Mexicans are Roman Catholic, and most villages host annual festivals in honor of their local patron saint. There is also a holiday to celebrate the Virgin of Guadalupe (see page 108), the patron saint for the entire country, and an 'untouchable' institution, along with the army and the president. Mexico's street life is colourful, with the *zócalo* (main square) its focus. Enjoying a rich tradition of feasting and festivals, Mexicans know how to enjoy life and even celebrate death during 'The Day of the Dead' (see 'Festivals & events', page 108). Many people live in vibrant, modern cities, but scattered along the coast are several unspoilt fishing villages, and inland are mountain settlements where life has changed little in the last hundred years.

● *Traditional Mexican Indian dress*

INTRODUCTION

INTRODUCTION

Valladolid's magnificent convent of San Bernardino de Siena

INTRODUCTION

The best of Cancún & the Riviera Maya

BEACHES

Most visitors come here with the intention of whiling away the days on the beautiful beaches that are found along the Caribbean coast, relaxing on the cool white sands and swimming in the the clear turquoise waters. The big, brash resort of **Cancún** (see page 16) is awash with luxury hotels, while nearby **Playa del Carmen** (page 42) and the island of **Cozumel** (page 60) are more laid-back. **Isla Mujeres** (see page 27) and **Puerto Morelos** (see page 36) are, by comparison, sleepy. Surfing and water sports are options in many locations, while beyond the main resorts lie plenty of pristine beaches where you can snorkel among manta rays and turtles and encounter seals lounging on the sand.

GIANTS OF THE SEA

The waters off Cancún and the Riviera Maya are fertile breeding grounds for **bottlenose dolphins**. There are aquatic theme parks where you can see them perform in Cancún, Isla Mujeres, Puerto Aventuras and Cozumel, but these awe-inspiring creatures are best seen in the wild – half of all captive dolphins die within their first two years and the rest last an average of just five years, instead of the usual 45.

BOAT TRIPS

Whether you are in a **glass-bottomed boat** surrounded by tropical fish, or taking to the high seas in a pirate vessel, opportunities for boat trips abound in Mexico. Take a lively **sunset cruise boat** with music and cocktails, or make a day tour to a nearby island.

JUNGLE VISITS

While the beaches are amazing, huge areas of lush vegetation can be found right behind them, and these can be explored from any resort in the area. From Playa del Carmen, you can **quad-bike** through the jungle and swim in **natural wells** on a jungle tour (see page 44).

INTRODUCTION

CITIES WITH HISTORY
Although it is best known for its beaches, the Yucatán Peninsula is rich in colonial history. Mérida's **Spanish cathedral** and Valladolid's wonderful **convent** (both on page 86) are historical highlights. If you decide to visit the capital, Mexico City boasts grand palaces and a main square lined with impressive buildings such as the **Catedral Metropolitana** (see page 91), which is one of the biggest churches in the world.

ARCHAEOLOGICAL SITES
Mexico's ancient sites are some of the most spectacular anywhere in the world. Just outside Mexico City is the ancient ruined city of **Teotihuacán** (see page 78), which in its heyday was one of the biggest in the world.

Each year, thousands of Cancún's visitors make a day of it at **Chichén Itzá** to marvel at the temples, pyramids, palaces and observatories built by the Mayans deep in the jungle (see page 75). A lesser-known but equally impressive site is **Cobá** (see page 77), within easy striking distance of any resort on the coast, or the beautiful cliff-top settlement of **Tulum** (see page 80), just 20 km (12½ miles) south of **Akumal** (see page 66).

WONDERFUL NATURE
Xcaret (see page 82) is a delightful park combining nature, history and entertainment. It includes beaches, rivers, a butterfly pavilion, a Mayan village and shows; **Xel-ha** is its sister park (see page 85). Experience both rainforest and savannas, with sightings of birds and big cats in the **Sian Ka'an Biosphere** (see page 82) or visit the island of Cozumel's **Chankanaab Park**, a marine conservation area where you can dive, snorkel and visit an aquarium (see page 61).

WORLD-CLASS SPORTS
Mexico's Yucatán offers some of the best scuba diving in the world, particularly off the island of Cozumel, where fishing opportunities are equally remarkable. The region also has world-class golfing (see page 60), including championship courses in stunning locations.

RESORTS
Places under the sun

HOTEL ZONE
CANCÚN TOWN
SEE PAGE 22
SIAN KA'AN
PUNTA BETE
AKUMAL
Río
Inglés
Laguna
del Amor
Laguna
Nichupté
PLAYA
LAS PERLAS
PLAYA LINDA
PLAYA LANGOSTA
SCUBA CANCÚN
PLAYA TORTUGAS
POK TA POK
GOLF COURSE
PLAYA CARACOL
PLAZA CARACOL
PUNTA CANCÚN
PLAYA
GAVIOTA
PLAYA
CHAC MOOL
PLAYA
BALLENAS
AQUA WORLD
BLVD KUKULCÁN
HILTON GOLF RESORT
EL REY
PLAYA
DELFINES
PARQUE
NIZUC
PUNTA
NIZUC
ISLA
MUJERES
GARRAFÓN
N

Cancún
party town

The story goes that in 1967, Mexican tourist officials were looking to build a new resort and their computer came up with Cancún as the perfect location. At the time, it was nothing but an offshore sand barrier, home to 100 Mayan fishermen. Two causeways were built to connect it to the mainland, and hotel after hotel sprung up along the 24 km (15 mile) beach, sandwiched between the sheltered lagoon and the Caribbean sea. With year-round sun, safe swimming, water sports, fishing, golf and plenty of hotels, beach bars, shops and restaurants, it's no wonder this has become Mexico's most popular resort – just as the computer predicted.

Cancún sits on the east coast of the Yucatán Peninsula, in the state of Quintana Roo. Just offshore is the longest coral reef in the Americas, stretching for 500 km (310 miles) along the coast. The Yucatán's major international airport is located here, as are consulates, doctors, major car rental companies and many other services. Cancún itself is divided into two areas: the **Hotel Zone** around the lagoon; and **Cancún City** (also known simply as 'downtown'), which started as a village for the workers of the tourism industry. The downtown area offers visitors a change from the beachfront Hotel Zone, with bustling markets, buzzing bars where Mariachi bands play, and some great restaurants and shops. Prices are also a bit lower and the ambience is more genuinely Latin.

THINGS TO SEE & DO
Game fishing ★
Cancún is a fishing paradise with barracuda, sailfish, marlin and tuna all on offer. To stand a good chance of catching a big fish, it's best to take an eight-hour charter at least. Try **Aquaworld** (❸ Blvd Kukulcán Km 15.2 ❶ 998 848 8327) for short tours. For all-day trips, night fishing and deep-sea tours, check out **Cancún Vista** (❸ Avenida Coba 31, Edificio Monaco, Oficina 2 ❶ 998 887 8069 ❼ www.cancunvista.com).

RESORTS

CANCÚN

Golf ★
The **Hilton Cancún Beach & Golf Resort** offers an immaculately kept, 18-hole, par 72 golf course, with a practice tee and putting green. At the time of writing, green fees were around £120 for non-Hilton guests, including the golf cart fee. ⓐ Retorno Lacandones Km 17 ⓣ 998 881 8016 ⓦ www.hiltonCancun.com/golf.htm

El Rey ★★
Towards the south end of the Hotel Zone, near the golf course, are the ruins of El Rey (The King). Inhabited from the 10th century AD until the beginning of the 16th century AD, its structures include plazas surrounded by buildings and several platforms that are connected by a long pathway. The site takes its name from a skeleton uncovered there, which was thought to possibly be a former Mayan king.

Snorkelling & diving ★★★
The waters around Cancún offer amazing opportunities for experienced divers, but with visibility in the water of up to 76 m (250 ft), even amateurs will have fun snorkelling. The best snorkelling area off the beach is near the Westin Regina, in the southern tip of the Hotel Zone. For most of the other places (Isla Mujeres, Cozumel, or some of the lagoon tours) you will need to sign up for a tour. Try **Scuba Cancún** for some of the best. ⓐ Blvd Kukulcán Km 5 ⓣ 998 849 7508 ⓦ www.scubaCancun.com.mx

Swim with dolphins ★★★
At the southern tip of the Hotel Zone is Parque Nizuc, home to the **Wet 'n Wild Water Park** (see page 105) and the ocean-fronted **Atlantida**, where you can learn all about bottlenose dolphins and then take a 30-minute swim with them in a sea enclosure. Cost is included in entry to the main park. ⓣ 998 881 3000 ⓦ www.parquenizuc.com

◀ *Aerial view of Cancún*

RESORTS

Tulum's cliff-top location has excellent sea views

BEACHES

The peninsular Hotel Zone is one long beach, with the lagoon on one side, and most hotels fronting the ocean on the other. The ocean side is the place to go for swimming and tanning, while jet-skis, kayaks and other rentals are on the lagoon side. One of the best things about Cancún is that the sand is crushed coral rather than crushed rock, so it stays cool underfoot even on the hottest days.

The flat, sandy seabeds and shallow waters of **Playa Caracol** and **Punta Cancún**, at the northern end of the Hotel Zone, are perfect for children. **Playa Langosta, Playa Las Perlas** and **Playa Tortugas** feature all kinds of beach games and diving and snorkelling tours, as well as regular shuttles to the island retreat of **Isla Mujeres** (see page 27). And, of course, there are plenty of bars and restaurants.

The beaches on the east coast benefit from the ocean breeze, but have bigger waves. **Playa Ballenas** is a great place to people watch, and tube rides, volleyball and parasailing will keep you amused. The views

CANCÚN

from **Playa Delfines** and **Punta Nizuc** are fantastic, and the latter is home to some of the more upmarket hotels.

> All beaches in Mexico are public property, so don't be put off choosing your favourite in the Hotel Zone, even if it looks private.

Right at the southern tip of the Hotel Zone is a gem of a beach that can only be accessed by walking through the property of the **Camino Real Hotel** at Punta Cancún (the beach itself is public property). There are no hawkers, no music and no volleyball, which can be a welcome change.

South of Cancún, the beaches of **Punta Bete** (58 km/36 miles) and **Akumal** (100 km/60 miles) are both spectacular. Akumal in particular is renowned for its good snorkelling and diving (see page 66).

EXCURSIONS
Chichén Itzá ★★★

Don't miss any chance to visit this ancient Mayan city (see page 75). Most organized tours to Chichén Itzá depart around 08.00, and it is a three-hour trip to the site. Tours are advertised at most hotels, or you can book over the Internet (W www.chichen-itza-tour.com).

> There are cheap, comfortable hotels close to most of the main Mayan sites, so check-in the night before if you want to avoid the crowds on your visit. Many sites open at 08.00, but the tour buses arrive at around 11.00.

Sian Ka'an Biosphere (Where the Sky is Born) ★

This beautiful 1^1/$_2$ million acre (almost ^{2}/$_3$ million hectare) wildlife reserve (see page 82) includes rainforest, wetlands, savannas and marine environments. The biodiversity here stretches from tiny, colourful butterflies to families of howler monkeys, pumas, jaguars and tapirs. Among the 300 bird species in the reserve is the Jabiru stork, the world's largest bird capable of flight. **Ecocolors** offers a variety of tours (① 998 884 3667 W www.ecotravelmexico.com).

RESORTS

Tulum and Xel-Ha ★★★

From its cliff-top perch, the ancient settlement of **Tulum** (see page 80), 130 km (80 miles) south of Cancún, commands a terrific view of the Caribbean Sea. The largest building, El Castillo, may at one time have served as a lighthouse. Between this and the 'Temple of the Wind', a break in the steep cliff gives way to a beautiful beach of fine sand. The easy access to the sea supports the view that Tulum was a departure point for fishing and trading vessels and one of the main ports of the Mayan civilization..

Many of the tours leaving from Cancún are combined with a visit to nearby **Xel-Ha** (see page 85). This is a great spot for snorkelling, with thousands of brightly coloured tropical fish to see, and it's also a great place to relax.

CANCÚN

RESTAURANTS & BARS (see maps on pages 16 and 22)

You will never be short of dining options in Cancún. Every fast food outlet you can think of is here, as well as a host of fantastic restaurants serving good food in gorgeous settings. Prices in the Hotel Zone restaurants match the going rate in the USA, which means they are cheaper than the UK – downtown you will find some great bargains.

> While some of the cheapest and best restaurants are downtown, taxis from the Hotel Zone can be overpriced. Instead, catch the bus to the Chedarui supermarket – then hail a taxi to your restaurant of choice. Prices are very reasonable for both.

100% Natural €€ ❶ (see page 16) This is a great place for a healthy breakfast or lunch. The shakes and smoothies here are legendary, and there are plenty of vegetarian takes on traditional Mexican food. The setting is magnificent with huge plants and trees dotted around the outdoor dining area. ⓐ Plaza Caracol, Hotel Zone and Avenida Yaxchilán, downtown ❶ 998 884 3617

Club Grill €€€ ❷ (see page 16) Part of the elegant Ritz Carlton Hotel, this is the place to go for a romantic dinner and dance in Cancún. ⓐ Paseo Kukulkán Km 13.5 ❶ 998 881 0808

La Dolce Vita €€ ❸ (see page 16) A reasonably priced Italian favourite, with a fine selection of seafood and home-made pastas. ⓐ Blvd Kukulcán Km 14.6, opposite the Marriot Hotel ❶ 998 885 0161

La Habichuela €€ ❹ (see page 22) Over the past 30 years, this unmissable downtown restaurant has built up a solid reputation for its fine Caribbean food and the magical ambience of its Mayan garden area. ⓐ Margaritas 25, next to 'Las Palapas' Park ❶ 998 884 3158

La Parilla € ❺ (see page 22) Near Périco's, this is also popular with tourists and locals. The food is authentic and beautifully

23

● *Plantation House restaurant, Cancún*

prepared, while the superb margaritas, daiquiris and live music will keep the conversation flowing. ⓐ Avenida Yaxchilán 51 ⓘ 998 884 5398

Périco's €€ ❻ (see page 22) Fun is certainly on the menu at this downtown steakhouse. The prankster waiters will entertain the young children, and the food is simple but delicious. If you want to take away a souvenir, why not a bottle of tequila with your picture on it? ⓐ Avenida Yaxchilán 61 ⓘ 998 884 3152 ⓘ Live *mariachi* show; gets busy, so try to book ahead

Plantation House €€€ ❼ (see page 16) Jutting out into the lagoon, this high-class restaurant serves dishes such as duck medallions in green-pepper sauce. ⓐ Blvd Kukulcán, Km 10.5 ⓘ 998 883 1433 ⓘ Reservations necessary; smart dress advised

CANCÚN

Señor Frog's € ❽ (see page 16) After 20.00 there is a cover charge here, which includes a cocktail of your choice. Mix in the regular contests, DJ's and karaoke sessions, and you are in for a noisy evening of fun. Standard menu of steaks, burgers and Mexican staples.
ⓐ Kukulcán Km 9.5, La Playa Chac Mool ❶ 998 883 1092

Winners Sports Bar € ❾ (see page 16) In the heart of the party district, this is where to see that crucial Premiership football match, although most of the time, the plasma screens will be showing US sports. ⓐ Party Central Km 9.5 ⓦ www.winnerssportsbar.com

NIGHTLIFE (see map on page 16)

Cancún lives to party. Most hotel bars spill out onto the beach and are open until late, and then the party really starts at the huge superclubs and bars that are spread throughout the **Hotel Zone**. American college students come here in droves during their 'spring break', from late February to the middle of March, when the clubs are at their busiest.

You could do worse than start your evening with some cool drinks and reggae at the **Terrasta reggae bar** ❿ (ⓐ Blvd Kukulcán Km 9.5 ❶ 998 883 3333). **Coco Bongo** ⓫ is large, loud and crowded and the dance music is interspersed with mini-shows and trapeze acts. Sizeable queues form after midnight (❶ 998 883 5061). With a capacity of 3500, **La Boom** ⓬ is one of Cancún's biggest venues. All drinks are included in the admission price, but the waiters still expect to be tipped for prompt service. Sounds are rave, RnB and techno, with an adjacent hip-hop bar (❶ 998 849 7587). **Dady'O** ⓭ is among the best clubs in Cancún, with first-class sound and lighting technology and a spectacular 3D laser show. The club has five bars and a snack bar (ⓐ Blvd Kukulcán ❶ 998 883 3333).

Many of the hotels have deals with bars and clubs, and may offer you a wristband for free entry or discounted drinks. Cheap buses run the length of the hotel strip all night. Have small change ready, and just give the driver a nod when you want to get off.

RESORTS

Next to the Dady'O nightclub, is the **O Ultra Lounge** ⑬, part of the same franchise, but with a more laid-back atmosphere, fine cocktails and good DJ sets (ⓐ Blvd Kukulcán Km 9.5).

If it's all about the music, then **The City** ⑭ is the place. Cancún's newest club plays host to big-name DJs from around the world, and – if you can believe it – has capacity for beach parties of 15,000 (ⓦ www.thecitycancun.com).

SHOPPING

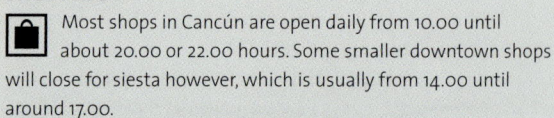

Most shops in Cancún are open daily from 10.00 until about 20.00 or 22.00 hours. Some smaller downtown shops will close for siesta however, which is usually from 14.00 until around 17.00.

Plaza Caracol at the northern end of the strip is one of many shopping plazas in the hotel zone, offering fashion boutiques, art galleries and jewellery shops (ⓐ Blvd Kukulcán Km 8.5).

Downtown, you are more likely to find a bargain, and certainly more authentic shopping opportunities. **The Ki Huic Open Air Market** (ⓐ Avenida Tulum, downtown) is the city's oldest crafts bazaar. Here you'll find goods such as leather, pewter, carved wood, pottery, hammocks, rugs, baskets, and traditional Mexican clothing items like *huaraches* (sandals) and *huipiles* (colourful, embroidered Mayan dresses).

Another famous market is the downtown **Mercado 28**, but many will find the market holders here to be a little too pushy, and despite its big reputation, goods are often overpriced.

For food shopping, casual clothing, shoes, beach towels and sun cream, Cancún's downtown supermarkets are the cheapest option. Most open at 07.00 and close at midnight, although **Walmart** is open 24 hours a day. To get there from the Hotel Zone take the bus Ruta no. 15 and ask the driver to drop you off at the Walmart bus stop.

ISLA MUJERES

Isla Mujeres
island retreat

Only a short ferry-ride from the brash, high-rise hotels of Cancún, the tiny Isla Mujeres is nonetheless a million miles away in atmosphere. Francisco Hernández de Córdoba, the first European to visit the Yucatán, gave the island its name – which means 'Island of Women' – when he came ashore in 1517 and found clay statuettes of partially-clad women.

Although it has now been discovered by tourists, Isla Mujeres retains much of its sleepy, fishing village charm and is still cheaper than Cancún. It is only 8 km long and 2 km wide (5 x 1 ¼ miles), but the island is home to some fantastic beaches and fine restaurants. Its setting is tropical, with a sea that is turquoise blue and warm all year round. There are plenty of activities to keep the whole family amused and the regular fast ferry to the mainland makes it a great base for exploring the Riviera Maya. There are good snorkelling areas and some of the better swimming beaches are to the south along the western shore. The ferry docks, town and most popular beach, **Playa Cocoteros**, also known as **Playa Norte** and **Nautibeach**, are at the northern tip of the island. It's easy to find your way around the grid of narrow streets in the town and there is a main plaza that also serves as a basketball court just inland from the ferry docks.

THINGS TO SEE & DO
Dolphin Discovery ★
This company offers a variety of programmes where you can swim with dolphins in a marine enclosure, or get into the water with docile sharks and stingrays kept in tiny enclosures. ➌ Laguna Mar, Sac Bajo ➊ 998 849 4757 Ⓦ www.dolphindiscovery.com

El Garrafón Eco Park ★★
At the south end of the island, Garrafón is packed with quirky activities, both in the water and on land. You can explore underwater with 'Snuba'

Isla Mujeres Map

Legend
1. ARTESANIAS ARCO IRIS
2. DE CORAZON
3. BAHIA DIVE SHOP
4. TOBACCO & CO

Locations

- Playa Norte
- Zazil-Ha
- Baño del Rey
- Hidalgo
- Lopez Mateos
- Juarez
- Av. Matamoros
- Av. Abasolo
- Madero
- Morelos
- Nicolas Bravo
- Allende
- Avenida Rueda Medina
- Sea Wall Walk
- Faro
- Passenger Ferry
- Auto Car Ferry
- Islote Chico
- Bahia De Isla Mujeres
- Isla Tiburon
- Salina Chica
- Sac Bajo
- Dolphin Discovery
- Laguna Makax
- Caribbean Sea
- Salina Grande
- La Gloria
- Turtle Sanctuary
- Playa Paraiso
- Hacienda Mundaca
- Playa Lancheros
- Playa Indios
- El Garrafón Eco Park
- Arrecife Manchones
- Faro
- Punta Sur
- Temple of Ixchal

(similar to scuba diving, but with the air tanks on a floating raft above you) and 'Sea Trek' where a special helmet allows you to walk along the sea bed. You can also hire snorkelling gear and glass-bottomed sea kayaks. On land, attractions include a zip line ride, observation tower, climbing pole, snack bars and a restaurant. In the afternoon, the park becomes busy with Cancún day trippers. ⓐ Km 6 Garrafón-Punta Sur ⓘ 998 849 4950 ⓦ www.garrafon.com

Hacienda Mundaca ★★
Constructed by Fermín Mundaca, a notorious pirate and slave trader, the hacienda and its magnificent gardens were intended to house the unrequited love of his life, a local girl who preferred a younger man to the brutal, old corsair. It drove Mundaca slowly mad, and he died alone in distant Mérida, leaving behind his tomb in the Isla Mujeres cemetery, complete with engraved skull and cross bones. The hacienda and gardens are (slowly) being restored and now a zoo has been added with snakes, birds, monkeys and the odd big cat. ⓐ Near Playa Lancheros

Turtle Sanctuary ★★★
Always a hatching ground for the area's giant sea turtles – once killed for their meat and shell and their eggs dug up for food – the sanctuary is now a haven for these animals that continue to lay their eggs in the soft sand here every May until September. The turtles are now under government protection and their eggs are placed in pens to keep them safe – hatchlings are then placed in tanks until they are large enough to be released into the wild. A visit here is an uplifting experience.
ⓐ Laguna Makax, Sac Bajo ⓘ 998 877 0595 ⓒ Open 09.00–17.00

BEACHES
The sands on the west coast of the island are the most popular – despite the calm waters and good facilities, they are still uncrowded compared to Cancún. The windward side is even less developed, though the surf can sometimes be a little rough. **Playa Norte**, is the most popular beach on the island and within easy reach of town. Kayaks, snorkelling gear,

RESORTS

lounge chairs and beach umbrellas can all be rented for a reasonable amount, and there are plenty of low-key beach bars where you can while away the hours with a cocktail under a thatched roof. **Playa Paraiso** and **Playa Lancheros** on the south-west coast of the island offer peaceful swimming in crystal clear waters. **Playa Indios** is an exclusive beach situated near **Casa O's** restaurant (see page 33).

Many of the boats on day trips from Cancún land on the island for lunch, so you may want to make a retreat for a few hours to avoid the crowds.

EXCURSIONS
Bird watching ★
North of Isla Mujeres, the tiny island of Isla Contoy is around 8 km (5 miles) long and is barely 20 m (22 yds) across at its widest point. Home to over 70 bird species, including brown pelicans, roseate spoonbills, herons, kingfishers and cormorants, it also sees flocks of flamingos arrive in April. The best months to spot turtles burying their eggs in the sand at night are June, July and August. The island can be reached by a 45-minute boat trip from Isla Mujeres, but visitor numbers are restricted, so advance booking is recommended. Contact **Contoy Express Tours** (❶ 998 877 1367) for details of tours. Further afield is the **Sian Ka'an Biosphere** on the mainland (see page 82), a huge nature reserve where over 300 bird species have been counted.

Mayan ruins ★★★
Although the remains of a temple to the Mayan goddess, Ixchal, can be found on the south tip of the island, the cliff-top ruins have suffered hurricane damage, and the main draw here is now the view. On the mainland coast, the ancient Mayan settlement of **Tulum** is soaked in history (see Excursions, page 80). It's also possible to visit the spectacular ruins of the Mayan city of **Chichén Itzá** (see page 75) in one day, although overnight tours are also possible. Contact **Viajes Prisma** (ⓐ Avenida Rueda Medina 9C ❶ 998 877 0938) for tour details.

ISLA MUJERES

● *View from the southern tip of the Isla Mujeres*

RESORTS

Beach bars provide drinks, snacks and a break from the sun

ISLA MUJERES

RESTAURANTS (see map on page 28)

Casa O's €€ ❶ With its thatched roof and open sides it might look like a basic *palapa*, but a fine wine list, delicious seafood and friendly staff make this a contender for the best restaurant on the island. The lobster bisque is a must. ⓐ Calle Garrafón ⓣ 998 888 0170 ⓦ www.casaos.com

Casa Rolandi €€€ ❷ Part of the Villa Rolandi hotel complex, fine international cuisine is served in a lovely location overlooking the Caribbean. ⓐ Fracc Laguna Mar SM7 Mza. 75 ⓣ 998 877 0700 ⓦ www.villarolandi.com ⓛ Open 08.00–23.00

La Cazuela € ❸ Great for brunch or late breakfast omelettes accompanied by good coffee and fresh juices. ⓐ Next to Mirador Tortugas, Sea Wall Walk ⓛ Open 07.00–14.00

Cocina Económica Carmelita € ❹ The cheapest lobster on the island, but still great. Set meals in a cosy family atmosphere. ⓐ Calle Juárez 14 e/ Bravo y Allende

Elements Of The Island € ❺ Trendy coffee house specializing in fresh juices and healthy breakfasts for a good start to the day. ⓐ Avenida Benito Juárez 64 e López Mateos y Matamoros ⓣ 998 877 0736 ⓦ www.elementsoftheisland.com ⓛ Open 08.00–13.00

Rolandi's Pizzeria €€ ❻ Popular member of the Rolandi family, with decent pizzas and pasta, plus seafood and fish dishes. ⓐ Avenida Hidalgo 110 ⓣ 998 877 0429 ⓦ www.rolandi.com

Zahil Ha €€ ❼ Delicious Mexican fare combined with pasta and seafood in a beachside haven that is part of the Na Balam beach complex. ⓐ Calle Zazil-Ha 118, Playa Norte ⓣ 998 877 0279 ⓦ www.nabalam.com ⓛ Open 18.00–23.00

RESORTS

ISLA MUJERES

NIGHTLIFE (see map on page 28)

You won't be kept awake by endless loud disco music in Isla Mujeres. What you will find are pleasant bistros, laid-back beach bars and low-key venues playing good music in a friendly atmosphere. **Playa Sol** ❽ is the best beach bar for a sunset cocktail (ⓐ Playa Norte). Also on Playa Norte, the hotel bar at **Na Balam** ❾ draws a crowd until midnight and there is live music at weekends. At **Bar Om** ❿ you can pour your own draft beer at your table and listen to jazz, reggae and latin music (ⓐ Calle Matamoros). **La Peña** ⓫ with a roof terrace overlooking the sea, draws a relaxed, late-night crowd, for dancing and playing pool (ⓐ Avenida Guerrero, opposite Church Square). For a fine margarita after midnight, head to **La Adelita** ⓬ where over 150 varieties of tequila are on sale (ⓐ Avenida Hidalgo 12A). **Nitrox Disco Club VIP** ⓭ is a brash newcomer (ⓐ Avenida Guerrero 11 ⓛ Open until 03.00, with ladies' night on Wed).

SHOPPING

Isla Mujeres has most of the same choice of handicrafts, clothes and jewellery that you see in the mainland tourist shops, but they are often cheaper. You will find the usual branded T-shirts, but without the word 'Cancún', 'Cozumel' or even 'Isla Mujeres' splashed all over them. Many of the tourist shops are around the ferry dock area and there is a supermarket at the east end of town. Visit **Artesanias Arco Iris** (ⓐ Avenida Hidalgo e/ Juarez) for silver, stones, and handicrafts such as blankets with intricate Mexican designs. **De Corazon** (ⓐ Avenida Abasolo e/ Hidalgo y Guerrero) is a small boutique stocking locally-made cosmetics, jewellery, scented candles and crochet goods. For snorkelling or dive equipment try the **Bahia Dive Shop** (ⓐ Avda Rueda Medina 166) and for fine Cuban cigars to bring back home try **Tobacco & Co** (ⓐ Avenida Hidalgo 14, Plaza Rocateliz).

◀ *A boat rests in the calm waters off Isla Mujeres*

RESORTS

Puerto Morelos
step back in time

This quiet and peaceful village, well away from the main road, is frequently compared to the Playa Del Carmen of 20 years ago. The locals still make a living from the sea, and visitors can enjoy a genuine Mexican experience at prices that put nearby Cancún to shame. Puerto Morelos is a perfect place for a relaxing beach holiday, and its location – halfway between Cancún and Playa del Carmen – means you can sample some great nightlife – but only if you feel like it.

The community, a mix of locals and foreigners, works hard to protect Puerto's status as a National Marine Park and keep development to a minimum. The focus of the village is the *zócalo* (main square) where you will find a handful of shops, bars, restaurants and a dive shop. A few steps away is an unspoilt, natural beach next to a small pier where fishermen bring ashore their daily catch for the village restaurants. From the pier, you can expect to be offered excursions to the reefs.

THINGS TO SEE & DO
Crocodile zoo ★★★
Just north of the village is **Croco Cun**, a zoological park that raises crocodiles and is home to monkeys, parrots, deer and other wildlife. The biologists that run the park have collected specimens of many of the reptiles that are indigenous to the area. An informative guided tour, which includes a visit to the reptile house and a sometimes hair-raising walk through the jungle (look out for the snakes, tarantulas and wild pigs), lasts 90 minutes. You may even get to handle a baby crocodile. There is a restaurant on site. ❸ Carretera 307, Km 31 ❶ 998 884 4782 ❶ Open 08.30–17.30 ❶ Make sure you wear insect repellent

Diving & snorkelling ★★★
The coral reef directly offshore is shallow – only 3 m (10 ft) at its deepest point, and snorkellers must wear a life jacket in order to remain near the

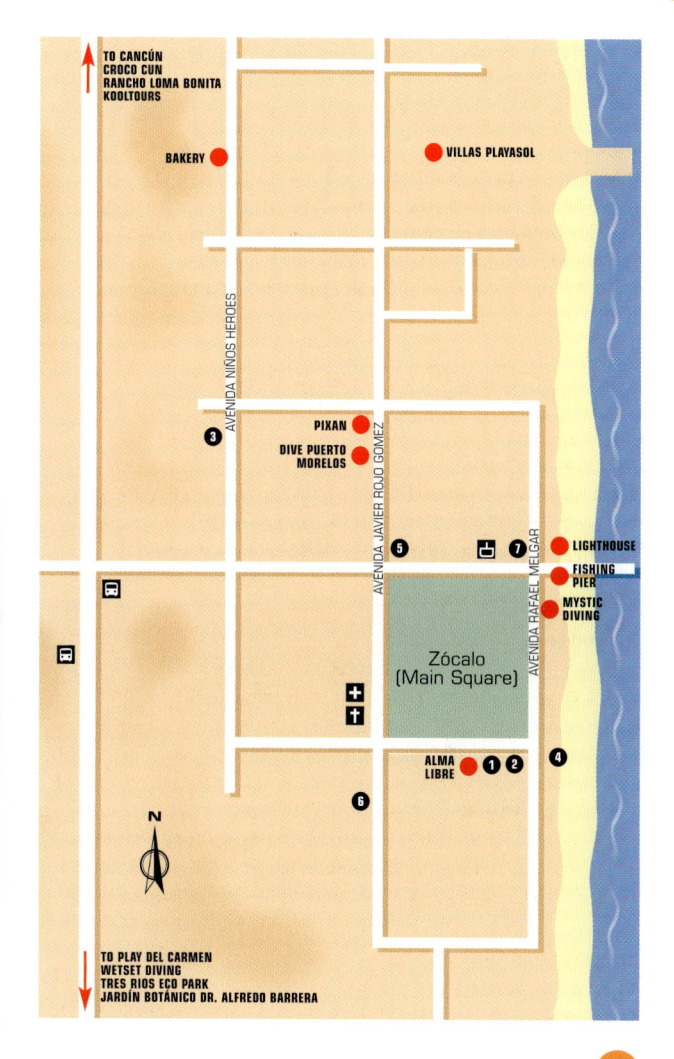

PUERTO MORELOS

surface and avoid it. Visual delights include iridescent darting fish, eels, rays and even the odd turtle. Puerto Morelos really is a mecca for divers with fantastic cave dives, wall dives and open-water excursions to amuse beginners and experts alike. Victor Reyes at **Mystic Diving** (998 871 0634) takes small groups out on tank dives and is a qualified PADI and NAUI instructor. Another experienced instructor, Paul Hensley, operates **Wetset** (998 871 0198 www.wetset.com) or you can try **Dive Puerto Morelos** (998 206 9084). All three companies offer English-speaking instructors and guides.

Jardín Botánico Dr. Alfredo Barrera ★

The relaxing walking trails of this 50-hectare park will delight avid gardeners as well as those who just feel like a change from the beach. Precious hardwood trees, wild orchids, medicinal herbs, and cacti of all shapes and sizes abound. Visitors often spot wild deer, spider monkeys, parrots, toucans and other birds. Carretera 307, Km 33 Open 09.00–16.00 Bird-watchers admitted earlier on request; remember to check you have insect repellent with you and wear long trousers

Rancho Loma Bonita ★★

This is one of the few places where you can arrange horse riding on the beach. Or you can choose to go quad-biking around a circuit that takes in the beach, jungle and mangroves. Tours can be booked direct, or from many hotels. Carretera 307, Km 31 998 887 5465

Tres Rios Eco Park ★

Head south towards Playa del Carmen and at the halfway mark you will come across this nature park, named after the three rivers that run through it. Despite its billing, it really is more of an outdoor leisure park, with water sports, horse riding and football all on offer. There is also a fine stretch of long, white sandy beach here. 998 887 8077 www.tres-rios.com Open 09.00–17.00

PUERTO MORELOS

BEACHES
Just offshore is a shallow coral reef (now a national park). As a result, the seabed close to the shore features a lot of sea grass. Nonetheless, the water is crystal clear and the reef makes for some great snorkelling just a stone's throw from the beach.

The main beach, which is larger than it once was following the hurricanes of 2005, is right behind the *zócalo*, and there are others to the south and north of the village. None of these are raked or manicured – except where hotel and restaurant owners choose to – but the beaches are clean, and devoid of the crowds and litter you might see elsewhere.

EXCURSIONS
Fishing ★★
Just ask around the pier and you will find sport-fishing boats for hire for up to four people. A cheaper alternative is to negotiate with the locals and take one of the smaller, local fishing boats. High season is from March to August. Each May, an international tournament is held, with fishermen from around the world hunting the tuna, blue marlin and barracuda that can be found beyond the reef.

Jungle tour ★★
Kooltours take small groups on one- and three-day tours, where you can discover crystal clear *cenotes* (natural wells), freshwater lagoons and hike to the cultural wonders left behind by the Maya – a world away from the bus-tour experience of Cancún. ⓐ Hotel Rancho Sak Ol ⓘ 998 101 7696 Ⓦ www.kooltours.com

RESTAURANTS (see map on page 37)

Café del Puerto € ❶ Great for vegetarian sandwiches and fresh juices. ⓐ Avenida Tulum, opposite Pelicanos

Hola Asia €€ ❷ With a chef who grew up in Hong Kong, this little place offers a wonderful selection of Chinese, Japanese,

RESORTS

Thai and Indian cuisine. Don't miss General Tso's Chicken – a local culinary legend. ⓐ On the *zócalo* (main square) ⓣ 998 871 0679 ⓦ www.holaasia.com ⓛ Open Mon–Sat 17.00–23.00, Sun 15.00–23.00

John Gray's Kitchen €€ ❸ Near the hotel Inglaterra is this relaxed gourmet restaurant with soft jazz and a varied menu that is always changing. Very popular. ⓐ Avenida Niños Heroes ⓣ 998 871 0449 ⓛ Open 17.00–23.00 ⓘ Reservations recommended

Los Pelicanos €€ ❹ With its ocean view and fine seafood menu, this is a great place for a dinner and is popular for cocktails. ⓐ Behind the *zócalo* ⓣ 998 871 0014

El Pirata € ❺ An open-air snack bar selling *enchiladas*, hot dogs, hamburgers and sandwiches. ⓐ Avenida Javier Rojo y Zócalo

Posada Amor €€ ❻ An all-round winner that serves breakfast, lunch and dinner in a relaxed family atmosphere. The Sunday brunch buffet is something of an institution. ⓐ Avenida Javier Rojo Gomez ⓣ 998 871 0033

El Tio € ❼ This cheap and cheerful lunchtime diner is popular with locals and serves great chicken soup and local specialities like *sabutes*, *panuchos* and *tamales*. ⓐ Avenida Rafael Melgar, opposite the lighthouse ⓛ Closed evenings

NIGHTLIFE

When it comes to all-night partying, visitors can go to Cancún or Playa del Carmen. But before you head off, take a walk down to **La Caverna**, where local musicians gather to jam. Occasionally you may find a live band has blown in – just follow the noise. Come full moon, the locals may build a bonfire and throw a beach party.

◗ *Puerto Morelos is a mecca for diving*

PUERTO MORELOS

SHOPPING

The village has a general shop, off-licence, chemist and ATM. In addition, **Alma Libre** on the *zócalo* is probably the best English-language bookshop in the whole of the Yucatán, offering everything from the classics to the latest blockbusters. It is also a great place for local maps. ⓐ Zócalo ⓣ 998 871 0713 ⓛ Open Tues–Sun 10.00–15.00 and 18.00–21.00 (Oct–June)

Try **Pixan** for unique crafts, scented candles, stationery and other gifts. ⓐ Avenida Javier Rojo Gomez

RESORTS

Playa del Carmen & Playacar
relaxed resorts

Much smaller than Cancún, Playa del Carmen 64 km (40 miles) to the south has a somewhat European atmosphere. Little over a decade ago, 'Playa' – as it is affectionately known – was just a fishing village, but today it is one of the fastest growing communities in Mexico. A large international community holidays here, as well as a significant number of Mexicans and day-trippers. In addition, enormous cruise ships dock here twice a week, swelling the local population.

❶ BOUTIQUE MANGO
❷ MAYAN ARTS GALLERY
❸ AMBER MEXICANO & LA CALACA

PLAYA DEL CARMEN & PLAYACAR

Both Playa del Carmen and adjoining Playacar are centrally located on the Riviera Maya, roughly half way between the big, brash resort of Cancún and Tulum's scenic, cliff-top Mayan fort. The ancient Maya appreciated the area's charms centuries before the Spaniards arrived in the 15th century and way before the tourists got here. Mayan ruins dot the coast, with a large concentration around Playa del Carmen.

In the centre of town is the pedestrianized **5th Avenue**, which runs through an area of boutique shops, good restaurants and interesting native architecture. At its heart is the *zócalo*, or main square. West is **Avenida Juarez**, where the bus station, post office and a number of banks are located. North of 5th Avenue is where you will find most of the hotels, restaurants, bars and shops.

To the south is the purpose-built, gated **Playacar** development, with its 18-hole golf course, large all-inclusive resorts, private rental apartments and residential area. Surrounded by some small Mayan archaeological sites, and with a few attractions of its own, it is still just a five-minute taxi ride from here to Playa del Carmen.

The further you walk away from 5th Avenue, the cheaper the restaurants and shops become and the quieter the beaches are. The Avenues are numbered, 5th, 10th, 15th, etc., so although, for example, 30th may sound far away from 5th, it's only a short walk.

THINGS TO SEE & DO
Diving ★★
Try diving in underwater caves, among dramatic stalactites, stalagmites and stunning coral formations with **Dive Mike** (❸ Calle 8, between 5th Avenue and Zona Federal Maritima ❶ 984 803 1228 ❿ www.divemike.com). There are also plenty of other dive shops to choose from in Playa del Carmen.

Golf ★★
Playacar boasts Yucatán's coast best golf course – the **Playacar Club de Golf**. This Robert Von Haggae-designed, par 72 championship course has

been sculpted out of the dense Mayan jungle, which makes for both scenic and challenging games. As an all-inclusive golf resort, any food or drink consumed is included in the green fee. Residents of certain nearby resorts can claim a discount, but because the rates change frequently, it is best to make enquiries at your hotel at the time of booking and again on arrival. Rates are reduced for twilight games (after 14.00). Ⓦ www.palace-resorts.com/playacar-golf-club

> It can get terribly hot on Playacar's course, so you are advised to play either early or late in the day.

Jungle Tour ★★
Drive a quadbike through the jungle, swim in a clear, 60-foot deep *cenote* (a natural well) and climb ancient Mayan ruins on a two-hour tour. **ATV Explorer** ⓐ Federal Highway 307 ⓘ 984 873 1606 Ⓦ www.atvexplorer.com

Xaman-Ha Aviary ★
Visitors can walk along trails surrounded by colourful birds, including parrots and toucans, flamingos and scarlet macaws as well as other wildlife such as iguanas and butterflies. ⓐ Paseo Xaman Ha S/N Fraccionamiento, Playacar ⓛ Open 09.00–17.00

BEACHES
Basking in the middle of the Riviera Maya, which stretches south of Cancún all the way down to Tulum, Playa del Carmen and Playacar have fine, white sand and crystal clear water. The beaches shelve gradually from the shore, making the sea seem like a large swimming pool.

Most of the resort's hotels are on or parallel to the coast, where the white sand is beautifully clean. The pretty, long sweep of the main beach of Playa del Carmen, with its bars and restaurants, narrows and then gets progressively quieter to the north. Beyond the big yellow hotel of Porto Real, lies a wider stretch of sand where you can rent an umbrella and a beach chair from one of the beach clubs. About a 10-minute walk

PLAYA DEL CARMEN & PLAYACAR

Playa del Carmen – from fishing village to secret hideaway

RESORTS

The long sweep of beach at Playa del Carmen

PLAYA DEL CARMEN & PLAYACAR

further north is **Coco Beach**, where there are a couple of restaurants and a few dive shops. Nearby **Chunzubul reef** provides both decent snorkelling and protection for local boats. Be aware though, that much of the coral near to the shore here has been destroyed.

All Playa del Carmen's surrounding beaches are open to the public, with various access points along the shore. However, access becomes more difficult the further north you travel, where right of entry through private property is limited. The best way to explore is on foot along the sand, as most of the roads leading from the main highway to the shore between Puerto Morelos and Playa del Carmen are gated driveways.

After the main beach, the initial stretch to the north is named after resorts – Playa Tukan, Mamitas, Shangri-La, Zubul and Coco beach. Bars and restaurants line this section of coast, so you need not walk far for refreshment. In addition, lifeguards are present, although safety precautions should always be followed.

Those with children might like to go to the part of the beach in front of the **Porto Real Resort**. A tiny section of coral here creates small pools of warm water often populated with small fish that are both safe and interesting for small members of the family.

Further north again are some of the most prized beaches on the Riveria Maya – the aptly named **Playa del Secreto** (Secret Beach) and **Playa Paraiso** (Paradise Beach), which are both 5 km (3 miles) wide. Sea turtles and crabs make regular visits to these big white stretches of nearly deserted sand. They quickly merge into the beaches of **Punta Maroma** and **Punta Bete**, featuring both limestone and jungle, which seem designed for relaxing.

EXCURSIONS
Cozumel ★★★
Take a boat trip to the beautiful island of Cozumel (see page 60), little over half an hour away. Easily visited on a day trip, it is a haven for divers and nature lovers.

RESORTS

Fishing ★
Although fishing trips on small *pangas* – either full or half day – are available by boat from the beach in Playa del Carmen, a much wider choice, on bigger boats, is on offer from Puerto Aventuras' marina, just 20 minutes south. These usually include (it's worth checking) a captain and mate, bait, tackle, fish filleting and light refreshments.

This part of the coast is particularly good for deep-sea fishing because the nearby island of Cozumel forces big fish to run close to the shore. Potential impressive catches include sailfish (high season Mar–July, but available year-round) and bill fish (Mar–Sept). Blue and white marlin are common, and tuna and reef fish can be caught all year.

Swim with dolphins ★★★
Swim and play with bottlenose dolphins at Parque Nizuc and learn about their behaviour from knowledgeable trainers. Participants must be at least 1.2 m (4 ft) tall and children must be accompanied by an adult (max. two children per adult). ⓐ Parque Nizuc, Cancún Hotel Zone (see page 17)

RESTAURANTS (see map on page 42)

Los Almendros €€ ❶ This small, rustic, family-owned restaurant offers traditional Yucatán food at very affordable prices.
ⓐ Corner of 10th Avenue and 6th Street

Byblos €€€ ❷ Elegant French restaurant complete with linen tablecloths. Escargot, French onion soup and lobster medallions in cream sauce are all on the menu and there is a good wine list.
ⓐ Between 5th Avenue and 10th Avenue, on 14th Street ⓘ 984 803 1790
⏱ Open Mon–Sat 18.00–01.00, closed Sun

Da Gabi Ristorante €€ ❸ Choose from Italian dishes such as oven-baked pizza and homemade fettuccini or go for fresh seafood or a T-bone steak. ⓐ 12th Street at 5th Avenue

PLAYA DEL CARMEN & PLAYACAR

Java Joe's € ❹ A local institution. Excellent coffees, from espressos to iced mochas, as well as pastries, sandwiches and bagels. ⓐ 5th Avenue between 10th and 12th Street ⓦ www.javajoes.net ⓛ Open 06.00–23.00

The Lazy Lizard €€ ❺ A friendly café where you can enjoy international and Mexican food in a pretty spot with almond trees. ⓐ 5th Avenue between 2nd and 4th Street ⓛ Open 07.00–23.00

Media Luna €€€ ❻ One of Playa's most popular restaurants offers beautifully prepared seafood, pasta and vegetarian dishes in an attractive setting. ⓐ 5th Avenue between 12th and 14th Street ⓣ 984 873 0526

Pancho's Mexican Café €€ ❼ International food served in a tropical garden patio by very friendly staff. ⓐ 5th Avenue and 12th Street

Sabor! € ❽ Pastries, coffees and vegetarian health foods are prepared and served by the owners. ⓐ 5th Avenue, between 2nd and 4th Streets

Tacos Arabe € ❾ Basic but good value, with excellent tacos. ⓐ Corner of 15th Avenue and 10th Street

Yaxche Maya Cuisine €€€ ❿ An award-winning restaurant that works with the local Mayan community. It offers a unique menu that is a fusion of Maya, Yucatán and European cuisine, and also holds special events and theme-dinner nights. ⓐ 8th Street, between 5th and 10th Avenue

Zas €€€ ⓫ With the same owners as Media Luna, this is similar but slightly more upmarket. ⓐ 5th Avenue, between 12th and 14th Street

RESORTS

NIGHTLIFE (see map on page 42)
Many of the restaurants in Playa del Carmen double as bars and nightclubs later in the evening. The 5th Avenue 'strip' is full of bars and clubs.

Deseo Lounge ⓬ has a roof-top bar with small pool, a DJ playing ambient music – and beds. The drinks aren't cheap, but at least they are brought to you while you remain horizontal (ⓐ 5th Avenue and 12th Street). **Alux** ⓭ (pronounced Ah-loosh) is a unique bar, restaurant and club built inside a cave, complete with water, stalagmites, live music and shows (ⓐ Juarez Avenue, three blocks west of Highway 307 ⓛ Open Tues–Sun, closed Mon ⓘ Cash only).

Chill out in the Moroccan lounge or on the bamboo beach beds of the **Blue Parrot** ⓮ while you listen to live music, fire dancers and DJs (ⓐ Calle 12 ⓦ www.blueparrot.com). **Tequila Barrel** ⓯ is friendly, and a great place for people watching, with more than 100 different tequilas to choose from (ⓐ 5th Avenue between 10th and 12th).

SHOPPING

Most of Playa del Carmen's shops are on the bustling pedestrianized main strip that runs parallel to the beach: 5th Avenue (also known as 'Quinta Avenida'). Popular items are jewellery, hammocks, panama hats and embroidered clothing.

Boutique Mango is an established clothing and accessories shop that focuses on resort wear and Mexican handmade creations (ⓐ 5th Avenue, between 6th and 8th Street), downstairs from Hotel Lunata. Nearby, with more clothing as well as crafts, is **Mayan Arts Gallery** (ⓐ 5th Avenue between 6th and 8th). **La Calaca** has a good collection of wooden masks and carvings (ⓐ 5th Avenue at 5th Street) and **Amber Mexicano** sells amber jewellery that is made by a local designer (ⓐ 5th Avenue between 4th and 6th Street).

In Playacar, the two main centres for shopping are **Paseo del Carmen** and **Plaza Playacar**.

PUERTO AVENTURAS

Puerto Aventuras
discreet development

Just 15 minutes from Playa del Carmen, and conveniently located for exploring the Riviera Maya, Puerto Aventuras is a gated development that is a world away from the bigger resorts on the coast. This 900-acre (365-hectare) private facility has been constructed around a large marina, complete with beach club, international restaurants, dive centre and nine-hole golf course.

Known simply as 'Puerto' by locals, the contained community prides itself on its 24-hour security. It is safe to walk or drive around at night, street sellers are controlled, and you will find none of the rowdy behaviour often on display in the nearby resorts of Playa del Carmen and Cancún. With just a handful of larger hotels, much of the accommodation is to be found in apartments and villas, all of which makes Puerto Aventuras popular with families.

THINGS TO SEE & DO
CEDAM Shipwreck Museum ★★
Navigating this stretch of coast has always been notoriously dangerous due to the Great Maya Reef offshore. This museum shows treasures found on 18th-century shipwrecks. ⓐ Behind the marina ⓘ 984 873 5000 ⓛ Open 10.00–13.00 ⓘ Free entrance; donations welcome

Golf ★
The small nine-hole course here is set in lush jungle that provides a cool relief from the heat of the day. Rental clubs and carts are available and there is a putting green. **Club de Golf y Tennis** ⓐ Behind the marina ⓘ 984 873 5109 ⓘ No reservations required; credit cards not accepted

Marina ★★★
The marina here is the biggest on the Riviera Maya and it is the only deep-water facility on the mainland between Cancún and Belize City.

RESORTS

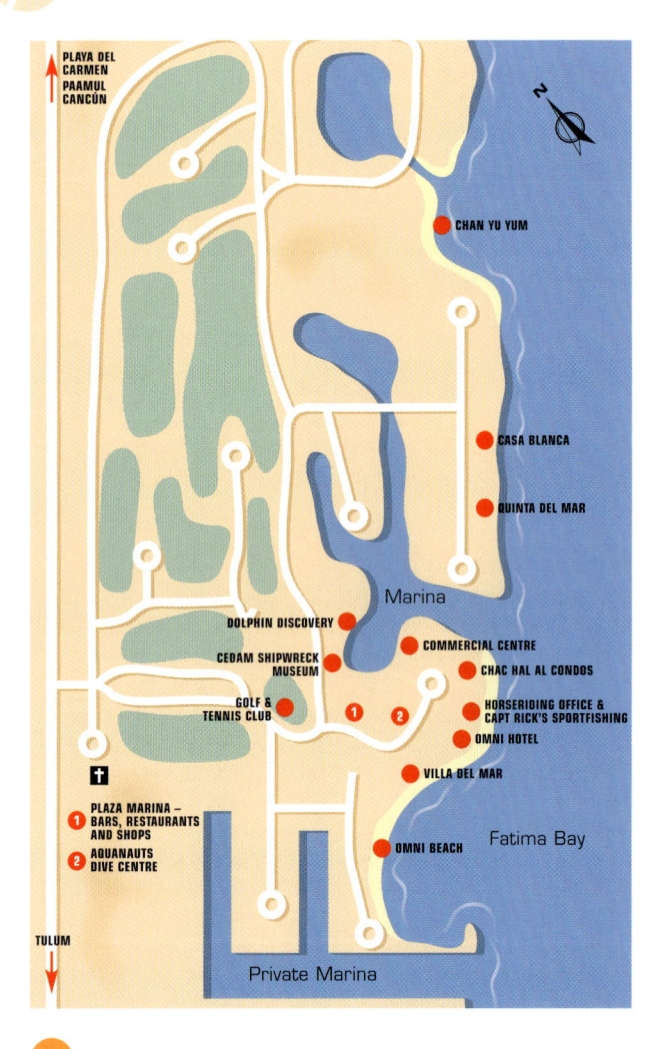

PUERTO AVENTURAS

Stroll around the pretty oceanfront location, stop for a coffee or something stronger, or even charter a boat. Choose a leisurely sail on a catamaran, or go snorkelling in the clear waters of the nearby beaches and coves nearby. Most tours include lunch and time for relaxing.
❶ 984 873 5108 Ⓦ www.puertoaventuras.com/marina/marina.htm

Parasailing ★
Take a gentle, uplifting ride pulled by a boat along the coast. ❸ Trips are offered daily from the marina ❶ 984 873 5108 ❶ Reservations are required

Tennis ★
Active types can play on synthetic grass courts surrounded by attractive vegetation at the resort's golf and tennis club. Discounted weekly and monthly rates are available and lessons can be arranged. **Club de Golf y Tennis** ❸ Behind the marina ❶ 984 873 5109 ❶ Open 08.30–dusk

BEACHES

The development of Puerto Aventuras is made up of two sheltered coves with powdery white sand. **Fatima Bay** at the centre of the resort covers more than 2.5 km (1½ miles) of shore from the Chac Hal Al hotel to the Grand Peninsula hotel. This wide expanse of beach with calm waters and a nearby reef, boasts various water sports and activities. Here, the Omni Hotel serves as a beach club, open to anyone who buys a drink.

To the north is the smaller **Chan Yu Yum** with the all-inclusive Sunscape Puerto Aventuras hotel (formerly the Oasis); access to the beach is restricted to guests staying in the immediate area. **Chac Hal Al** to the south is an inlet that forms a nature reserve with mostly exclusive accommodation.

Further afield, half way to Xcaret, is **Paamul**. This peaceful beach is perfect for relaxation and those who want to dive or participate in water sports. Nature lovers will appreciate the sea turtles who come here to lay their eggs between May and July.

RESORTS

PUERTO AVENTURAS

EXCURSIONS

Cancún ★★

This mega-resort is less than an hour away. Make a trip for a larger-than-life experience, but don't expect much relaxation (see page 16).

Cozumel ★★★

This nearby island is easily accessible, with daily departures from the marina. Cozumel's beaches and rich underwater life are the main attractions, particularly the diving and snorkelling (see page 60).

Diving ★

With the reef little more than 90 m (100 yds) from the beach, diving opportunities are not far away. The first wall, only 20 m (66 ft) deep, offers a variety of underwater sites with plenty to see. The more adventurous can venture onto a second wall that drops 40 m (130 ft) and even further. Several dive shops in the resort offer daily ocean reef diving, equipment rental and diving classes from beginners to master level. Try **Aquanauts** ⓐ Marina, Puerto Aventuras ❶ 984 873 5041 ⓦ www.aquanauts-online.com ⓛ Open 08.30–17.30

Fishing ★★★

Puerto Aventuras is a world-class centre for sport fishing, home to enticing catches such as sailfish, marlin, and dorado (mahi mahi), barracuda and tuna. Success is virtually guaranteed, partly thanks to the proximity of the grounds to Puerto Aventuras itself. Those who opt for the more leisurely pursuit of bottom fishing can look forward to reeling in Snapper. Both full and half day trips are available from

---

Most fishing trips will accommodate non-fishers, who can snorkel and swim from the boat. At the end of your fishing trip, ask the crew to fillet your catch – you can take it home for supper.

◀ *Relax by the pool at the exclusive Puerto Aventuras marina*

RESORTS

Capt. Rick's Sportfishing. ⓐ Marina, past the OMNI Hotel on your right ⓘ 984 873 5195 ⓦ www.fishyucatan.com ⓛ Open 08.00–17.00
ⓘ Credit cards accepted

Horse riding ★★
Take a gentle, scenic ride through the jungle, then swim or snorkel (equipment provided) in the cooling waters of *cenotes* (natural wells), enjoy a picnic lunch and spot butterflies and iguanas. The whole trip takes four hours door to door, available through **P.A. Stables**.
ⓐ On the right past the OMNI Hotel ⓘ 984 873 5035
ⓦ www.pastables.com/puerto.htm ⓘ Credit cards not accepted

Playa del Carmen ★★
Just 15 minutes to the north, this lively resort is worth a visit for its selection of restaurants and shops, or for change of scene (see page 42).

Swimming with dolphins ★
Dolphins as well as two manatees – Romeo and Juliet – can be seen in captivity at **Dolphin Discovery**. ⓐ Marina, Puerto Aventuras
ⓘ 998 849 4748 ⓦ www.dolphindiscovery.com ⓛ Open 09.00–18.00
ⓘ Advance booking recommended; credit cards accepted

Tulum ★★★
These spectacular, cliff-top ruins are just 25 minutes to the south of the resort (see page 80).

RESTAURANTS & BARS (see Plaza Marina on map, page 52)

Arigato €€ Only fresh fish bought that day from local fisherman will do for the owner of this excellent, beachfront sushi restaurant. Curries, salads and sandwiches are also sold.
ⓐ Behind the Marina, Plaza Marina Edificio C Loc. 3 ⓘ 984 801 0196
ⓛ Open 13.30–22.00 ⓘ Credit cards not accepted

▶ *Dolphins abound at Dolphin Discovery*

PUERTO AVENTURAS

RESORTS

Café Ole €€ This popular and friendly terrace café has a menu featuring everything from chicken chimichurri to high-quality steaks, with daily specials. On Sundays in high season, there is live music. ⓐ Opposite the Omni Hotel ⓣ 984 873 5125 ⓞ Open 08.00–23.00

Caribana € This simple place serves Mayan-inspired cuisine, including a great-value set-meal of soup, main course with salad and soft drink. ⓐ Behind the Italian Bakery, Plaza Marina Edificio A Loc. 8-A y B ⓣ 984 873 5175 ⓞ Open Mon–Sat 08.00–20.00, closed Sun ⓘ Credit cards not accepted

Dos Chilies €€ Good for a drink or snack and to watch the dolphins. ⓐ Plaza Marina ⓣ 998 841 6778 ⓞ Open 08.00–midnight

Golden Dragon €€ The Caribana restaurant (see above) transforms nightly into an Asian eatery serving mostly Chinese cuisine. Take out or eat in. ⓐ Behind the Italian Bakery, Plaza Marina Edificio A Loc. 8-A y B ⓣ 984 873 5175

Italian Bakery € This is *the* place for breakfast and it's not a bad spot for lunch and dinner either. ⓐ Off the Puerto Aventuras plaza ⓞ Open daily ⓘ Credit cards not accepted

SHOPPING

Those who are self-catering may want to visit one of the food shops in Puerto Aventuras, although Playa del Carmen has a lot more choice. Several boutiques and gift shops can be found around the marina. **Arte Maya** sells clothes and accessories created by a Mexican designer. **PA Boutique and Gift Shop** is more of a one-stop shop, selling everything from beachwear to postcards and film to snorkelling gear.

PUERTO AVENTURAS

Jones' Sports & Fun Bar €€ You will find American food and sports on several televisions both outside and inside, but British footie fans may also be able to catch the odd Premiership game. ⓐ Plaza Marina Edificio C No. 104, on the marina ⓣ 984 873 5381 ⓛ Open 11.00–23.00

Mediterraneo €€ Italian food and a full bar. Service is friendly but not always fast. ⓐ Plaza Marina Loc. 4-A, on the marina ⓣ 984 873 5418 ⓛ Open Tues–Sun evenings, closed Mon

Richard's Steak House €€ A basic diet of steak, seafood and pizza, along with a salad bar, is served up here, but specials and occasional barbecues may be worth a look. Some of the dishes are somewhat overpriced and the owner can be entertaining or annoying, depending on your point of view. ⓐ Plaza Marina Edificio E Loc. 3-B, on the marina ⓣ 984 873 5086 ⓛ Open for lunch and dinner

Taco Paco € Don't miss the Mexican food dished up at this much-loved roadside food stand. Owner Paco's seafood tacos are legendary. ⓐ Pemex station at entrance to Puerto Aventuras and Hwy. 307 ⓛ Open from 11.00, most days ⓘ Credit cards not accepted

NIGHTLIFE

No one really goes to Puerto Aventuras for the nightlife; if you are looking for late nights or discos, nearby Playa del Carmen is probably your best bet. That said, there are a handful of bars where you can enjoy a cocktail or a beer, some of which offer entertainment.

A good place to start is one of the thatched beachside **'palapas'** near the marina. **The Pub** on the marina, is really a restaurant, although it does have a good selection of beers as well as live music some nights. The **Pina Colada Jacuzzi Beach Bar**, part of the Omni Hotel, is in a scenic spot overlooking the Caribbean Sea and a great place for a tropical cocktail, but it does close at 19.00.

RESORTS

Cozumel
island paradise

Just 19 km (12 miles) from the coast, the island of Cozumel is surrounded by spectacular coral reefs that are home to thousands of tropical fish. Fringed by pretty beaches, oceanographer Jacques Cousteau introduced Cozumel to the world in 1961 and it has been one of the top diving destinations in the world ever since.

Understandably, many of the activities on the island are water-based, whether it is swimming in the clear blue waters, snorkelling over the reefs or taking a scenic boat ride. There is wonderful wildlife too and inland areas of jungle and mangroves.

Ferries from the mainland and large cruise ships dock in **San Miguel**, the only built-up area on the island. This small town is also home to almost all of the island's bars, shops and restaurants.

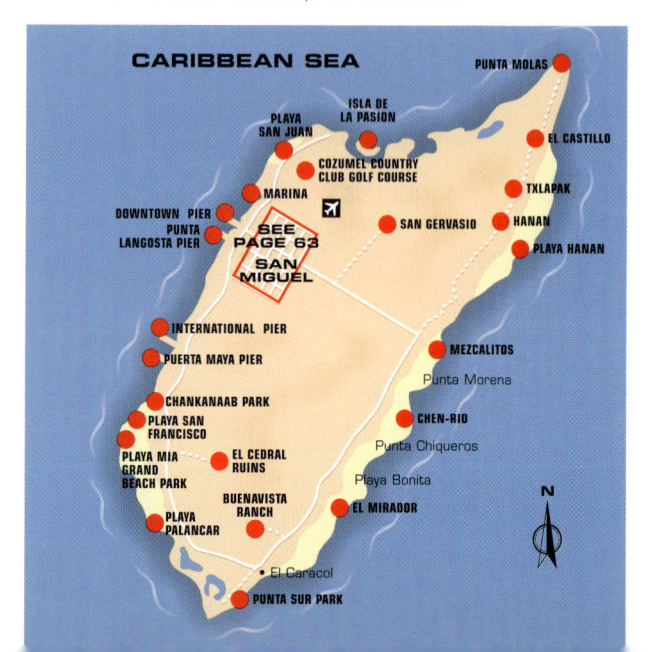

COZUMEL

THINGS TO SEE & DO

Boat Trips ★★

Drop 30 m (100 ft) beneath the waves and explore the reefs in the **Atlantis Submarine** (W www.atlantisadventures.com). Take a three-hour trip on a glass bottom boat to snorkelling spots or enjoy a sunset cruise, with music and cocktails.

Chankanaab Park ★★

Go diving and snorkelling and even swim with dolphins at this marine park and aquarium that features turtles, coral and fish. a Costera Sur Road Km 9.5 W www.cozumelparks.com.mx

---

If you love to snorkel, but are unsure about diving, why not try 'snuba', a combination of the two? Allowing you to breathe underwater, it is suitable for children over eight.

Diving ★★★

The island has world-class diving of all descriptions, whether you want lessons or specialized cavern trips. **Cozumel-Diving Net** is a website listing dive companies on the island (W http://cozumel-diving.net).

Fishing ★★

The island is a dream for those who love to fish. Go bone fishing for red snapper and grouper or take a deep-sea fishing trip and come back with marlin, dorado or tuna. The best fishing months are February to July.

Golf ★

The par 72 golf course at the **Cozumel Country Club** provides challenges for players of all handicaps, and is surrounded by mangroves and tropical rainforest. t 987 872 9570 W www.cozumelcountryclub.com.mx

Punta Sur ★★

A park and nature reserve set in a lagoon and marine environment, with mangrove jungles and white sand beaches where you can see all types

RESORTS

of flora and fauna, from crocodiles and iguanas to 220 species of birds.
Ⓦ www.cozumelparks.com.mx

Water sports ★★
A range of water sports is on offer at **Playa Mía Grand Beach Park**, from snorkel tours to parasailing. Children love the banana rides, water trampoline and 'beach iceberg'. Ⓦ www.playasol.com.mx

BEACHES
One continuous white sand beach stretches all around the island. The best snorkelling is on the western side, where equipment and facilities are offered by the many beach clubs. And if you buy a drink or two you can use the sun loungers and parasols. The beaches on the east face the open sea and are often deserted, although you will need transportation to get to them. One of the most beautiful beaches is **Playa San Francisco**. On the main part of the beach there are restaurants and water sports, but there is a quieter stretch a few miles south at **Playa Palancar**. North of San Miguel, **Playa San Juan** is the best place for swimmers and those keen on water sports.

EXCURSIONS
Playa del Carmen (see page 42) on the mainland can be reached in just 35 minutes on one of the fast boats. Or why not take a day trip to see the spectacular sacred site of Tulum (see page 80)?

RESTAURANTS (see map opposite)

The Diamond Café € ❶ Popular for breakfast croissants and muffins and lunchtime sandwiches, when service can be slow. Great coffee. ⓐ Avenida Rafael Melgar 131

French Quarter €–€€ ❷ Big portions of Cajun food are served inside or on the roof terrace. Try 'gumbo' or the house special of filet mignon with red-onion marmalade. ⓐ Avenida 5 between Calle Adolfo Rosado Salas and Calle 3 ⓣ 987 872 6321 ⓛ Closed for lunch

COZUMEL

- ① CRAFTS MARKET
- ② PUNTA LANGOSTA PIER
- ③ LOS CINCO SOLES
- ④ FORUM PLAZA

MAYAN HERITAGE MONUMENT
DIVER'S MONUMENT
FERRY PIER TO PLAYA DEL CARMEN
FLAG
NAVAL BASE
CHEDRAUI SUPERMARKET MALL / CONVENTION CENTER

SAN MIGUEL

AVENIDA CARLOS ANTONIO GONZALEZ
CALLE 14
CALLE 12
CALLE 10
CALLE 8
CALLE 6
CALLE 4
CALLE 2
AVENIDA BENITO JUAREZ (LEADS TO EAST COAST)
CALLE 1
ADOLFO ROSADO SALAS
CALLE 3
CALLE 5
CALLE 7
CALLE 9
CALLE 11
CALLE 13
CALLE 15
CALLE 17
CALLE 19
CALLE 21
CALLE 23

AVENIDA RAFAEL MELGAR
AVENIDA 5
AVENIDA 10
AVENIDA 15
AVENIDA 20
AVENIDA 25
AVENIDA 30
AVENIDA 35
AVENIDA 40
AVENIDA 45
AVENIDA 50
AVENIDA 55
AVENIDA 60
AVENIDA 65
AVENIDA 70

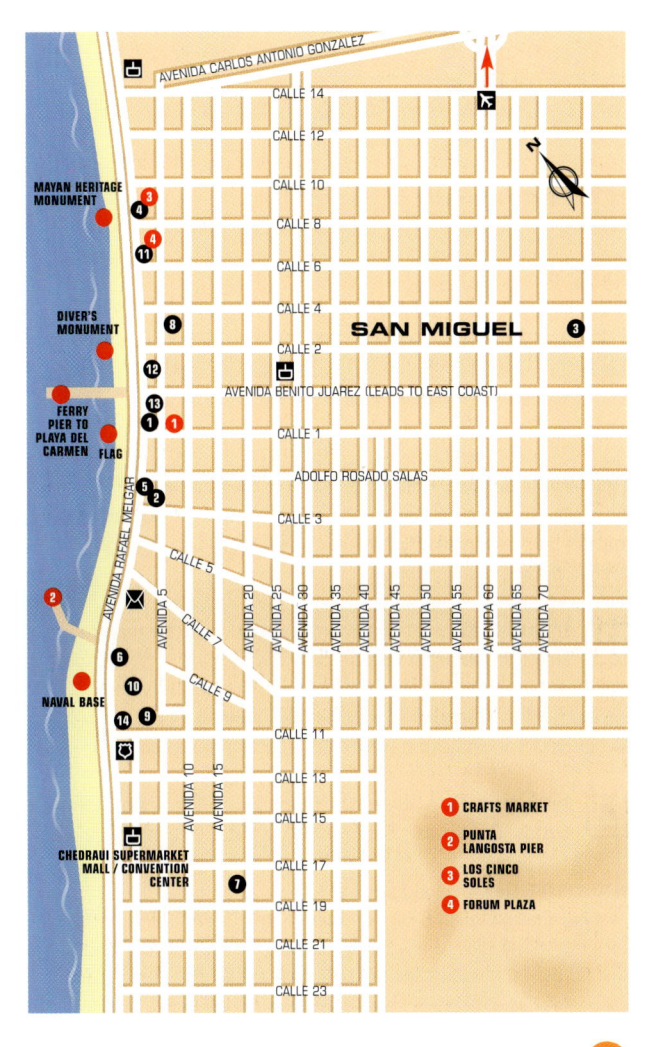

63

RESORTS

El Moro €€ ❸ People come to this great backstreet restaurant for the food and not the decor, which is very basic. Excellent Mexican dishes and seafood. The lime soup and lobster are particularly good. ⓐ Calle 75 Norte 124 ⓘ 987 872 3029

Pancho's Backyard €€ ❹ The beautiful courtyard makes this a romantic spot to eat. Mexican dishes, steak and seafood are served by friendly staff. ⓐ Los Cincos Soles Mall, Avenida Rafael Melgar 27 ⓘ 987 872 2141

Pepe's Grill €€-€€€ ❺ Large, popular place overlooking the bay, with live guitar music. Excellent grilled steaks and seafood and a children's menu. ⓐ Avenida Rafael Melgar at the corner of Salas ⓘ 987 872 0213 ⓘ Reservations recommended

Punta Langosta Mall € ❻ Opposite the Langosta pier, this shopping mall is home to a wide variety of fast-food restaurants such as Burger King (first floor), Subway and TGI Friday. ⓐ Avenida Rafael Melgar, between Calle 7 and 11

El Turix × ❼ Small restaurant located outside the main tourist area. Specializing in Yucatán cuisine, with Spanish, French and Lebanese influences. The *chicken pibil* baked in banana leaves is a speciality. ⓐ Avenida 20 Sur, between Calle 17 and 19 ⓘ 987 872 5234 ⓒ Closed Oct and lunch times ⓘ Credit cards not accepted

Zermaat € ❽ A bakery with delicious goodies, as well as fresh breads. ⓐ Avenida 5, between Calle 2 and 4

NIGHTLIFE (see map on page 63)

Evening entertainment begins and ends early here. Yet the nightclubs are pretty lively and friendly, many featuring live music. Most venues are just north of the main plaza on Avenida Rafael Melgar or in the Punta Langosta shopping centre. Some larger resorts have their own discos.

COZUMEL

Tequila Lounge ❾ is a chic bar with a fantastic location on the seafront. Watch the sunset while sipping a cocktail and listening to lounge music (ⓐ Avenida Rafael Melgar at Calle 11 ❶ 987 872 4421). **Carlos and Charlie's** ❿ is a lively, mainstream spot open until the early hours on the waterfront (ⓐ Punta Langosta Mall).

Aat **Havana Club** ⓫ go for live jazz, cocktails and Cuban or Mexican cigars but try and avoid the imported spirits, which are expensive (ⓐ Avenida Rafael Melgar 37-B between Calle 6 and 8 ❶ 987 872 1268). Visit **Joe's Reggae Bar** ⓬ for reggae dancing and salsa until dawn (ⓐ Avenida Rafael Melgar, at the ferry pier ❶ 987 872 3275).

Cactus ⓭ boasts a disco, live music and bar that stays open until 05.00 (ⓐ Avenida Rafael E. Melgar 145 ❶ 987 872 5799) while the **Neptuno Dance Club** ⓮ is Cozumel's most well-known and oldest disco, with a light-and-laser show to entertain (ⓐ Avenida Rafael Melgar at Calle 11 ❶ 987 872 1537).

SHOPPING

Thanks to the large cruise ships that visit Cozumel, there are lots of shops – chiefly selling clothes and jewellery. The main shopping areas are along the waterfront and from the ferry pier back towards the main town square, which is known variously as Plaza del Sol, Plaza San Miguel or just the Plaza! Behind this square there is a **Crafts Market** selling all kinds of souvenirs.

Many shops, particularly those near the cruise ship passenger terminal at **Punta Langosta Pier**, offer duty-free goods. These claim to offer large savings, but are often quite expensive, so be sure to compare prices.

There is a wide selection of crafts, as well as local jewellery and embroidered clothing, at **Los Cinco Soles** (ⓐ Avenida Rafael Melgar Norte 27 ❶ 987 872 0132). **Forum Plaza** has a range of shops selling clothes and designer goods, as well as an interactive jewellery workshop.

RESORTS

Akumal
natural beauty

This small resort, whose name means 'place of the turtle' in Mayan, lies in the heart of the Riviera Maya. Once a huge coconut plantation, Akumal began its tourist life way back in the 1950s when it was established as an exclusive centre for divers. The Mayan population was moved to a new town on the other side of the motorway, and today the community is one of the most Americanized on this stretch of coast.

Despite being the Riviera Maya's oldest resort, Akumal is still something of a secret and maintains a relaxed atmosphere. Its main attractions are the lovely beaches, spectacular lagoon and lush jungle. Abundant bird and animal life surrounds the resort, and can be spotted either on short walks and bike trips or on longer, organized tours.

THINGS TO SEE & DO
Akumal Kid's Club ★
Children up to ten years old can participate in either morning or evening activities, such as art, beach games and nature trips. ⓐ Akumal Bay near Lol-Ha Snack Bar ⓔ info@akumaldirect.com ⓛ Open 09.00–14.00 and 18.00–21.00 ⓘ Pre-paid day rates are cheaper; for more information

Bike rides ★★
Akumal is small enough to be explored by bicycle. Make a tour around the town, visiting beaches and the lagoon, or take a longer trip to the jungle. Bike hire available from **Travel Services Akumal** ⓐ Akumal Bay, by Akumal Dive Shop ⓣ 984 875 9030/31

Fishing ★★
Sport fishing is big in Akumal, where all fish are 'catch and release'. King fish, tuna, sailfish and marlin are popular hauls in the main season between April and July. Two-hour trips throughout the year

PLAYA DEL CARMEN
PUERTO AVENTURAS
CANCÚN

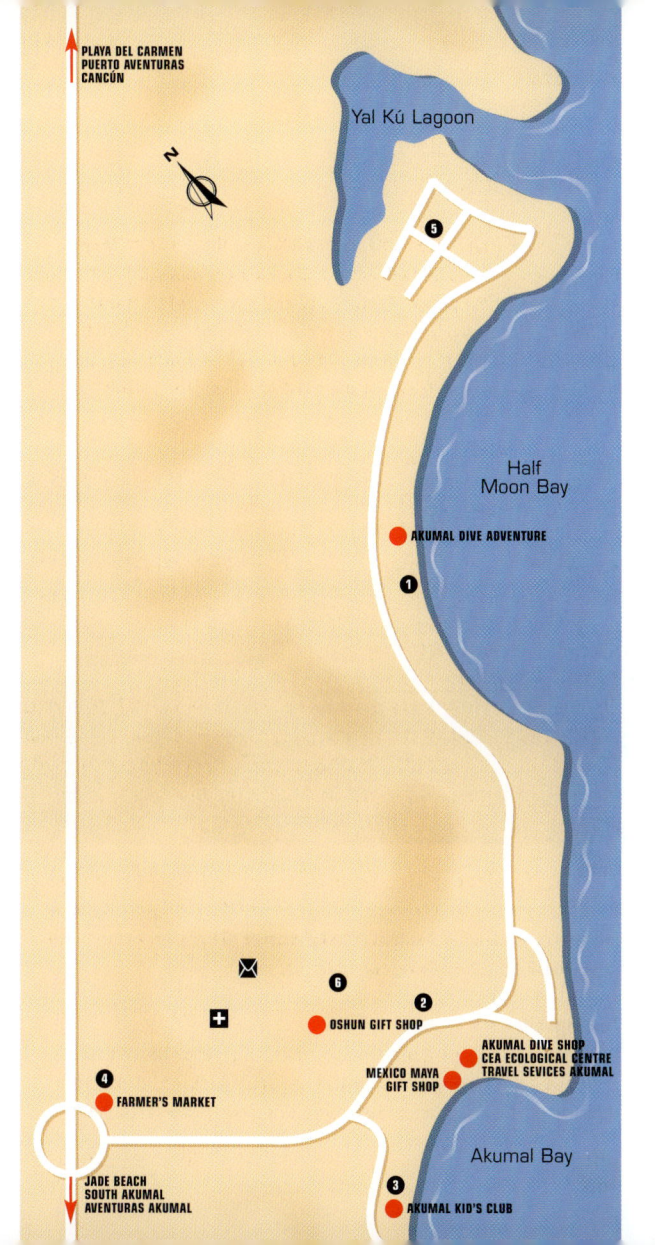

Yal Kú Lagoon

Half Moon Bay

⑤

① AKUMAL DIVE ADVENTURE

⑥
② OSHUN GIFT SHOP

AKUMAL DIVE SHOP
CEA ECOLOGICAL CENTRE
TRAVEL SEVICES AKUMAL

MEXICO MAYA
GIFT SHOP

④ FARMER'S MARKET

JADE BEACH
SOUTH AKUMAL
AVENTURAS AKUMAL

Akumal Bay

③ AKUMAL KID'S CLUB

RESORTS

● *Yal Kú lagoon's clear waters are a delight for swimmers and snorkellers*

are also possible with **Akumal Dive Adventure** ● 984 875 9157
● Open 08.00–17.00 ● Reservations advised

Turtle Walk ★★★
Enjoy the rare experience of seeing turtles land on the beach to dig their nests and lay eggs. You can also help biologists record important information and to protect these fascinating creatures. Turtle sightings

AKUMAL

are not guaranteed and even if you do encounter one it may take two hours before she returns to the sea, so patience is necessary. Wear insect repellent and shoes suitable for the beach and don't forget drinking water, and for evening tours, a torch. Make sure your hands are clean as you may be asked to help one of the creatures. ⓐ Centro Ecologico de Akumal ⓘ 984 875 9095 ⓛ Open Mon 14.00–18.00, Tues–Fri 08.00–14.00 and 16.00–18.00, Sat 10.00–14.00; walks Mon–Sat at 20.00 (May–Sept) ⓘ Make reservations, as group sizes are limited

Yal Kú Lagoon ★★

The clear waters of this narrow lagoon, sandwiched between dense mangroves and the sea, invite swimming and snorkelling. Birds such as pelicans and herons can be spotted on its tiny islands, while towards the mouth you may see stingrays and feeding sea turtles. This special place is also very fragile and is threatened by tourist traffic. ⓐ North Akumal, 2 km (1 mile) from Akumal Bay ⓛ Open 08.00–17.00 ⓘ Do not use sunscreen as it pollutes the aquatic life – if you burn easily, wear a T-shirt; entrance fee payable

---

Do a good deed and adopt a turtle for a few pounds from the CEA (Centro Ecológico de Akumal) at ⓦ http://ceakumal.org/adopt-a-turtle.html

RESORTS

BEACHES

The beaches around Akumal all have fine, white sand and a coral reef close to the shore, which makes for calm waters as well as good snorkelling. The focus of the resort is **Akumal Bay**, where there are good water sports and facilities. This beach can get very crowded during holidays and weekends. To the north, the quieter **Half Moon Bay** has a pretty, crescent-shaped beach with some rocks.

Even quieter is **Jade Beach**, a mile and a half south of Akumal Bay and reached by an attractive, easy 20-minute walk along the coast. The next beach south is **South Akumal**, a gated community of mostly beachfront villas. Finally, **Aventuras Akumal**, a lovely long stretch of beach, is four miles south of Akumal itself. The northern part of this beach has a hotel whose amenities are available for a fee.

EXCURSIONS

Cancún ★★

A little over 95 km (60 miles) away, this huge holiday resort with lots of entertainment is easily reached on a day trip (see page 16).

Cozumel ★★★

The ferry to the lovely island of Cozumel, known for its beaches and sealife (see page 60), leaves 32 km (20 miles) north of Playa del Carmen. A visit is easily possible as a day trip.

Diving ★★

Akumal has world-class diving, with varied options. Dive trips are easily arranged, whether you choose night diving, *cenote* (shallow cave) diving, or more straightforward reef diving. ⓐ Akumal Dive Shop ⓘ 984 875 9032 ⓦ www.akumal.com

---

The Akumal Dive Shop takes children (minimum age eight years) into water less than 3 m (10 ft) deep to explore the underwater world. The trips last for an hour.

AKUMAL

Puerto Aventuras ★
Just ten miles away, Puerto Aventuras offers activities such as golf, tennis as well as a marina (see page 51).

Robinson Crusoe Tour ★★★
There are several 'Robinson Crusoe' tours, all of which last most of the day, taking in a secluded bay for swimming, snorkelling and fishing and including a fresh fish lunch. ⓐ Akumal Dive Shop ⓘ 984 875 9032 ⓦ www.akumal.com ⓘ Reservations recommended

RESTAURANTS (see map on page 67)

La Buena Vida €€ ❶ The kitchen specializes in Caribbean, Mayan and seafood dishes. Lunch is served under thatched umbrellas on the beach. Outside are two crow's nests, which offer great views of the coast. The bar, with its sand floors and swings, is particularly popular late at night. ⓐ Half Moon Bay ⓘ 984 875 6061

Cueva Del Pescador €€ ❷ The 'Cave of Fish', which specializes in local cuisine, is deservedly popular. It is a great place for a cold beer or glass of wine and freshly grilled fish or seafood tacos. The food is good as well as being reasonably priced. ⓐ Next to Turtle Bay ⓛ Open daily for lunch and dinner, closed Sun in low season

Lol Ha Restaurant €€€ ❸ The longest running of all Akumal restaurants is still the most successful. The menu features seafood, steak and Mexican dishes and there is an adjoining pizza restaurant and beach bar serving snacks. Go for a Happy Hour at 17.30–18.30. ⓐ Akumal Bay ⓛ Open 07.30–22.00 ⓘ Entertainment several nights a week, such as live jazz or folkloric dancing

El Perico € ❹ This roadside taco stand dishes out tacos and other Mexican fast food to an eager public. ⓐ At the entrance to Akumal, by the motorway. ⓛ Open most mornings and evenings, usually closed in the afternoon after lunch ⓘ No credit cards accepted

RESORTS

Que Onda Restaurant €€ ❺ An intimate establishment in a lovely tropical jungle location near the Yal Kú Lagoon. Italian dishes and seafood are the specialities. ⏰ Open Wed–Mon 14.00–22.30, closed Tues

Turtle Bay Bakery € ❻ A delightful spot and the local favourite for breakfast such as homemade muffins, fresh fruit, or eggs cooked whatever way you like them. ⓐ Akumal Bay ⏰ Open Mon–Sun 07.00–15.00 and Tues–Sat 18.00–21.00

SHOPPING

For souvenirs, try any of the small, **open-air markets** along the main coast road, both north and south of Akumal. Look for hammocks, pottery and local crafts, and expect to bargain. Self-caterers may be interested in the **Farmer's Market**, which is open Wednesdays and Saturdays at the entrance to Akumal. It offers a wonderful variety of tropical fruits and fresh vegetables.

The **Mexico Maya Gift Shop** in Akumal Bay has a good range of gifts, including jewellery. Souvenirs and beachwear can be found at the **Oshun Gift Shop** (ⓐ On the left just, outside Akumal's main entrance).

EXCURSIONS
Out & about

EXCURSIONS

Pre-Hispanic culture

Way before the Spanish arrived, advanced cultures like the Aztecs and Mayans left their mark all over Mexico. Although it's impossible to see everything in one visit, the Yucatán makes a great base for exploring the country's rich history of ancient civilisations, particularly as there are some spectacular archaeological sites within easy reach of the main resorts along the Caribbean coast.

PRE-HISPANIC CULTURE

CHICHÉN ITZÁ

This site was an important commercial and ceremonial centre, believed to have been constructed between AD 600 and the end of the first millennium. The Maya were advanced mathematicians, engineers and astronomers, and this is evident in the buildings that remain here.
You can still explore the magnificent pyramid-shaped temple known as **El Castillo**, which was dedicated to the feathered serpent god Kukulkán. Some think that the snake that can be seen moving over the pyramid on both equinoxes (21 September and 21 March) was designed as a signal to begin the planting and subsequent harvest of crops.

Also not to be missed are the remains of the recreational **Jego de Pelota** ('Ball Court') which was larger than a modern football pitch with goals that were raised 6 m (19 ft) up in the air! It is believed that war-captives were sometimes forced to play, and although nobody knows if it was the winners or losers who were then sacrificed, we do know that their heads, along with countless others were displayed on spikes in the **Tzompantli** ('Wall Of The Skulls').

But we know that not all sacrificial victims ended up there. The **Cenote Sagrado** ('Sacred Well') is an impressive natural

Pyramid of Kukulkan in Chichén Itzá

EXCURSIONS

well, 90 m (98 yds) in diameter, within which explorers have found not just pieces of gold and jade jewellery, but even the skeletons of children. As you peer over the edge into the 20 m (65 ft) deep abyss, you can only imagine the horror the condemned faced before they were sacrificed to the rain gods. 170 km (105 miles; around three hours) from Cancún, on the road to Mérida Open 08.00-17.00 Buses depart frequently from Cancún and the main resorts along the Riviera Maya, mostly as part of organized tours; from Cozumel and Isla Mujeres, many tourists opt for a same-day flight package, which is almost as cheap and much less tiring

PRE-HISPANIC CULTURE

For the best experience, try to arrive at archaeological sites as early as possible (many open as early as 08.00), as they not only tend to get crowded from 11.00 onwards, but the heat of the sun can be unbearable in the middle of the day.

COBÁ

This hugely important Mayan site, dating from AD 600–900, covers more than 80 sq km (95 sq yds), and it is estimated that between 50,000 and 100,000 people lived here. The Mayan ruins at Cobá are unique in that they have not really been restored in any way – the jungle has just been cleared from around them. Only a few of its estimated 6,500 structures have been uncovered, but those that have been revealed are impressive and astonishingly beautiful. Experts believe that Cobá was probably an important trading post between the Caribbean coast and the inland cities.

It is a steep climb to the top of the **Nohoch Mul pyramid** (the tallest in the Yucatán at over 42 m / 138 ft) but the view from the top is well worth it. Mile after mile of jungle canopy is broken up only by **Lake Macanox** and the tops of temples and other pyramids jutting above the treetops – testament to the number of structural wonders still to be revealed. At the top of Nohoch Mul is a small temple with two small carvings that are echoed in the ruins at Tulum, though no-one is quite sure what their meaning is.

One of the most intriguing features of Cobá is the raised network of wide roads known as *sacbes* (white roads), which long ago stretched across the entire Yucatán Peninsula. Like Roman roads, these were built in straight lines from A to B, and they were constructed at a height of 1–2 m (3–6½ ft) above the ground. Up to 20 m (22 yds) wide, they were covered with limestone plaster and often included ramps and junctions. One of these ancient motorways stretches over 100 km (62 miles) from Cobá to Xahuna near Chichén Itzá. More than 50 *sacbes* have been discovered at Cobá, all originating at the central plaza and stretching out

◀ *Sunset at Chichén Itzá*

EXCURSIONS

in four general directions. ❸ 50 km (31 miles) west of Tulum ❹ Open 07.00–18.00 ❶ Regular tours run from Cancún, Playa del Carmen and the Riveria Maya, combined with a trip to Tulum's ruins, and shopping

> On visits to inland archaeological sites, it's always advisable to bring plenty of water, sunscreen and a hat, as the temperature and humidity are usually higher than on the coast. Wear a sturdy pair of shoes or boots if you want to explore the structures properly, and of course, don't forget your camera.

TEOTIHUACÁN

Those who opt for a few days in Mexico City will not want to miss this fantastic site, just 48 km (30 miles) north-west of the capital. Once the largest city in the Americas, Teotihuacán is considered by many to be the most important archaeological site in the world. At its height, the population of the city was greater than that of Rome. The city was built around the **Avenida do los Muertos** (the Avenue of the Dead). The third largest pyramid in the world is here – the imposing **Pirámide del Sol** (Pyramid of the Sun). At the other end is the **Pirámide de la Luna** (Pyramid of the Moon).

The area was occupied from around 500 BC for a thousand years, when it was abandoned. It was discovered six centuries later by the Aztecs. Because the city's founders did not leave a writing system, its origins and the true names of its features were never known. When the Aztecs established the site as a ceremonial ground, they gave the city its name, which means 'Place of the Gods'.

It was also the Aztecs who named the tallest structure the 'Pyramid of the Sun' because the front wall faces the exact point on the horizon, where the sun sets at spring and autumn equinoxes. This pyramid is 70 m (230 ft) high with a 220 m (241 yds) base. It was built around AD 150. The now nlkeutral stone façade was originally painted bright red. The smaller Pyramid of the Moon was built between AD 250 and 600.

❶ *Mayan ruins at Cobá*

PRE-HISPANIC CULTURE

EXCURSIONS

> **A BITE TO EAT**
> Out at the pyramids in Teotihuacán, **La Gruta** is a restaurant in a natural grotto that makes a great place to round off a visit to the Aztec site. JFK dined here. ⓐ Zona Arqueologica Teotihuacán ❶ 55 5956 0104/5956 0127 ⓒ Closes 19.00

At the entrance to Teotihuacán, keep an eye out for groups of men in traditional costume gathering around a tall pole. These are the **Voladores de Papantla** (Papantla Flyers). They climb the pole, one perches on top playing a flute and four others 'fly' down the pole, spinning around it, and supported only by a rope from their ankle. The show is repeated several times daily and the team passes a hat around for tips afterwards. ⓐ Teotihuacán is about 48 km (30 miles) north-west of Mexico City – about an hour's drive. Buses leave from the capital's north bus terminal every 30-60 minutes ⓒ Open Tues–Sun 09.00–17.00 ❶ Organized tours to Teotihuacán are available from Mexico City, either as part of a group on a bus, or in a private car that will give you added flexibility during your trip; many hotels based in Mexico City also arrange local tours to the pyramids that include transportation, food and a guided tour.

TULUM

These Mayan ruins perched on a cliff top overlooking the Caribbean are certainly not Mexico's biggest, but are arguably the most beautifully located. The walled fortress was built to protect Tulum, one of the main ports of the Mayan civilization. Don't miss the impressive tower, **El Castillo**, or **El Templo de los Frescos**. ⓐ 67.5 km (52 miles) south of Playa del Carmen ⓒ Open 08.00–17.00 ❶ Full day trips from Cancún and the resorts of the Riviera Maya usually combine a visit to the ruins with entry to the aquatic theme park **Xel-Ha**

▶ *Papantla Flyers are guaranteed to amaze onlookers*

PRE-HISPANIC CULTURE

EXCURSIONS

Jungles, rivers & wildlife

Should you tire of life on the beach, the Yucatán is home to a host of nature reserves, parks and attractions that showcase the enormous biodiversity this country has to offer.

SIAN KA'AN BIOSPHERE

This 1.5-million-acre wildlife reserve near Tulum includes rainforest, wetlands, savannas and marine environments. The wildlife here ranges from tiny, colourful butterflies to families of howler monkeys, pumas and jaguars. Among the 300 bird species in the reserve is the Jabiru Stork – the world's largest bird capable of flight. A good-value all-day tour can be booked directly with the park administrator, **Centro Ecológico Sian Ka'an** (W www.cesiak.org), which combines walking, swimming and boat-travel through the reserve.

It's free to drive through the reserve, but to get the most out of it, call **Friends of Sian Ka'an** (❶ 998 884 9583) to book a guided tour. They are a non-profit organization, so the money is ploughed back into the reserve.

If you are staying in Playa Del Carmen or Cancún, your guide will normally pick you up from your hotel. If you are coming from further afield, or want to spend more time in the reserve, you can book into the comfortable, on-site visitor centre. Alternatively, inclusive week-long tours with airport pick-up are offered by **Ecocolors** (❶ 998 884 3667 W www.ecotravelmexico.com). ❸ The reserve itself is situated three hours south of Cancún, past Tulum, on the road to Boca Paila and Punta Allen ● Open 09.00–21.00

XCARET

An hour's drive from Cancún, this natural wonder has been transformed into a popular theme park, with snorkelling and swimming tours through underground rivers as well as dolphin programmes, and spectacular evening shows that hark back to the glory days of the Maya. Don't miss the chance to see a tapir – a strange and rare beast that looks like a cross between a pig and an anteater. You might even

JUNGLES, RIVERS & WILDLIFE

'Jaguar Island' at Xcaret

EXCURSIONS

Snorkelling with tropical fish at Xel-Ha

JUNGLES, RIVERS & WILDLIFE

catch a glimpse of the big cats that roam around 'Jaguar Island'. You can arrange to be picked up from your hotel, and the cost will be added to your ticket. Visit the **Xcaret Information Centre** in Cancún's Hotel Zone (ⓐ Next to the Fiesta Americana Grand Coral, in Cancún ⓦ www.xcaret.com). A cheaper alternative is to get there by bus and pay on entry. Take a bus from your resort to Playa Del Carmen. From Playa Del Carmen, it's a short taxi ride or you can take one of the many buses. ⓐ Xcaret is 45 miles from Cancún, close to Playa Del Carmen. ⓛ Open 08.30–22.00

> Admission to the park is not cheap, so if you are going to visit, leave early and make a day of it.

XEL-HA

A group of coves, lagoons, rivers and mangroves make up this eco theme park where you can get close to nature. Swim with tropical fish in crystal-clear rivers, snorkel through the underwater caves or just hop on one of the free bicycles and explore. When it's time to relax, retreat to the beach, the spa, or one of the many restaurants in the complex. Although a trip to the park is often combined with a visit to the ruins in Tulum, there is plenty to keep you occupied here for a full day. ⓐ Xel-Ha is 121 km (75 miles) south of Cancún ⓦ www.xel-ha.com ⓛ Open 08.30–18.00 ⓘ If you are travelling by bus (they run frequently from the downtown bus station in Cancún and along the coast), take a bus towards Tulum and ask the driver to let you off at the road near the park entrance, a mile's walk away.

EXCURSIONS

Colonial history
away from the crowds

A trip to one of the Yucatán's old colonial towns makes a pleasant change from the hectic pace of the larger coastal resorts. The people tend to be friendlier, the pace is more relaxed and you will have more time to appreciate the real Mexico, as well as discovering more of its complex past.

MÉRIDA

The state capital of the Yucatán was built on the ashes of the Mayan city T'ho. Once the Spaniards had triumphed, they tore down the pyramids and built the **Catedral de San Idelfonso**, the oldest cathedral on the North American continent. Today, Mérida is a bustling city of one million people and the peninsula cultural centre. Either wander around the charming narrow streets and colonial building of the centre, or take a short bus or horse-drawn carriage tour to take in the city's lovely gardens and plazas. There are lots of hotels and restaurants of every class and price range and good transport available to any part of the peninsula. Mérida is busiest with tourists in July and August, when it is also very humid. Winter is a more pleasant, cooler time to visit.
ⓐ Mérida is around a five-hour drive from both Cancún and Tulum
ⓘ There are plenty of sightseeing trips available from either place

VALLADOLID

Pronounced 'bah-yah-doh-leed', this is a pleasant colonial town halfway between Mérida and Cancún. Founded in 1552, the city boasts the convent of **San Bernardino de Siena**, one of the most beautiful buildings of the colonial era. The **Cenote Dzinup** south of the town is a marvellous underground well with stalactites and vines, making for a spooky atmosphere, and you can swim in it too. ⓐ Valladolid is 40 km (25 miles) east of Chichén Itzá, between Mérida and Cancún, with regular buses departing from both cities ⓘ If you are driving, it is quicker via the toll road, but Highway 180 winds through a number of scenic villages

COLONIAL HISTORY

Mérida's Catedral de San Idelfonso

EXCURSIONS

Air tours
a different perspective

The Mexican novelist Carlos Fuentes said: 'To see Mexico from the air is to look upon the face of creation.' From the sky, you will get a unique view of the wonders of the Yucatán, whether soaring over the Caribbean islands or spotting Mayan ruins in the depths of the jungle.

● *Breathtaking views of the Yucatán coastline from the air*

AIR TOURS

PANORAMIC FLIGHTS
Mangroves, beaches and Cozumel ★★
Atlas Sky Tours offers short flights in an Ultralight aircraft. You and your pilot will fly low over the mangroves and beaches on the coast, and take in the island of Cozumel. ⓐ Next to the Xcaret eco-park ⓘ 984 871 4020
ⓘ Flights last 20 minutes to half an hour

> The views you can get from ultralight aircraft are stunning, so make sure you take your camera to get some great pictures from the air.

Playa del Carmen and the Caribbean Sea ★★
From Playa del Carmen, you can take a flight that gives you a bird's-eye view of the coast and a panoramic view of Playa del Carmen and the Caribbean Sea. Flights with **Aerosaab** last for 15 minutes, 30 minutes, 45 minutes or one hour. ⓐ Next to Playa del Carmen Airport, on Ave 20 at Calle 1 ⓘ 984 873 0804 ⓘ Open 07.00-19.30 ⓘ Flights do not include tax; an additional 10 per cent sales tax applies on each ticket

Holbox Island ★★
This tiny island northwest of Cancún is just 42 km (26 miles) long. It is separated from the mainland of Mexico by a shallow lagoon, which forms a sanctuary for thousands of flamingos, pelicans and exotic birds. Holbox is essentially a fishing community, where the streets are sand and cars are uncommon. The island's inaccessibility means it has so far been protected from mass tourism and its natural beauty has been largely unspoilt.

Flights to Holbox can easily be arranged from Playa del Carmen and Cancún. The trip takes in panoramic views of the Riviera Maya and Isla Mujeres. Tours include a boat trip to the even smaller Isla Pajaros (Island of the Birds), where thousands of flamingos and other birds feed. Other natural attractions include iguanas, horseshoe crabs and a wonderful array of wild plants. You may even be lucky to catch sight of dolphins swimming in the sheltered waters. Tours also include a fresh fish lunch,

EXCURSIONS

a visit to a mandolin factory and a walk around the main village. **Aerosaab** (see page 89 for details) runs day trips three times a week from Playa del Carmen. ❶ Bring your swimming costume, sunscreen and a towel, and wear comfortable shoes

PRIVATE CHARTER FLIGHTS

The company **Aerosaab** (see above) offers private charter tours to many parts of the Yucatán peninsula, including Mérida and Uxmal Ruins, Cancún and Isla Mujeres, and various other combinations. Its Cessna planes can accommodate four or five people for between US$280 and $350 (£155-£200) an hour at the time of writing. Rather than travel by bus for several hours, why not fly to Chichén Itzá in under an hour from Playa del Carmen, Cancún or Cozumel? This way you can get to these sights by mid-morning and avoid the crowds and the heat of the sun.

MEXICO CITY

Mexico City
a trip to the capital

Mexico City is a holiday destination in itself, but many visitors choose to spend a couple of days here before heading to one of the coastal resorts, or to break their stay on the beach with a two-day tour. As the ancient centre of the Aztec empire, the city was called Tenochtitlán, and was built on an island in the middle of Lake Toxcoco. After the Spanish defeated the Aztecs, they drained the lake, but the spectacular canals and 'floating gardens' of Xochimilco (see page 92) still remain.

THINGS TO SEE & DO

In the centre, the city is much like a grand European capital, with wide boulevards and large public buildings. The *zócalo*, officially known as the **Plaza of the Constitution**, is the hub of Mexico City. This massive public square was built as a testament to Spanish power in the New World, and grand buildings surround it on all sides. The **Palacio Nacional**, on the eastern side of the plaza, is the seat of the Mexican government.

Bosque de Chapultepec ★

This large park is the city's lungs, and offers a welcome respite if the pollution gets too much for you. At weekends, the city's families flock here. The grand castle that was once the residence of Emperor Maximillian is worth a look.

◀ *A tiled house in Mexico City*

91

EXCURSIONS

> ### SHOPPING
>
> You'll find plenty to buy in this city, much of it from all over Mexico. For clothes, antiques, art and much more wander around the Zona Rosa. In this area you'll also find a branch of **Fonart** (ⓐ Londres 136-A), a government-supported organization with shops throughout the country that sell quality handicrafts such as glassware, wall-hangings and ceramics. No bargaining is allowed because the government sets the prices, which are reasonable.
>
> A little more than 1 km (½ mile) south of the Alamedia, is La Ciudadela (The Citadel), an area where people come to shop at the nearby **Centro Artesanal y Mercado de Curiosidades market** and at the **open-air market** at the Plaza del Buen Tono. These two places sell handicrafts from all over Mexico, at prices that are fair even before you begin bargaining.
>
> North of Bosque de Chapultepec, **Polcano** is a swish shopping district packed with fashionable boutiques, cigar emporiums, jewellers and leather-goods stores. If you're looking for fine crafts, antiques and collectibles, try the **Bazar del Sábado** in the fashionable southern neighbourhood of San Angel – a Saturday market in a beautiful location.

Catedral Metropolitana ★★★
The huge church that overlooks the north of the *zócalo* is one of the world's biggest, the cathedral was constructed over a period of 200 years, and is home to 14 chapels. ⓐ Plaza de la Constitución, Centro Histórico ⓛ Open 07.00-19.00

Floating Gardens of Xochimilco ★★
In the south of the city is this large network of canals and islands, centred around the historic neighbourhood of Xochimilco. Visitors can hire one of the decorated boats, rather like Venice's gondolas, and enjoy

MEXICO CITY

Ceremonial dancers in Mexico City's zócalo with cathedral in background

EXCURSIONS

a leisurely afternoon cruise. At the weekend, the place is packed with locals, many of whom bring their lunch to eat in the boats. *Mariachi* musicians who board the *trajineras* (as the boats are known) add to the atmosphere.

> The best view of Mexico City is from the top of the **Torre Latinoamericana**. This 44-storey skyscraper is four blocks east of the *zócalo*. There is an aquarium on the 38th floor (supposedly the world's highest!) and indoor and outdoor viewing platforms above.
> ⓐ Madero and Lázaro Cárdenas, Centro Histórico ⓛ Open 10.00–23.00

A BITE TO EAT

Arrive early at **La Nueva Opera** to enjoy great Mexican food at reasonable prices while you soak up the atmosphere in a comfortable booth. Legend has it that Pancho Villa rode in on his horse and fired his gun at the ceiling – you can still see the bullet hole (ⓐ Cinco de Mayo 10, Alameda ⓛ Closed Sun night). For a special meal, make for **Fonda Santa Clara**, a traditional Mexican restaurant. Make sure you reserve for dinner, as the restaurant is often full (ⓐ Avenida San Jerónimo 775 ⓣ 55 5557 6144 ⓛ Closed Sun and Mon evenings).

The city's cantinas are no longer for men only, and the atmosphere in **Cantina La Guadalupana** is welcoming and fun. Open since 1928 and steeped in history, this is a great place to enjoy a beer and tapas (ⓐ Higuera 14, Coyoacán ⓛ Closed Sun). Sanborn's **Casa de Azulejos** is a beautiful building with an exterior façade of elaborate stonemasonry and mosaic tiles. Have lunch in the courtyard and admire the architecture, or go upstairs for a cozy drink and meal (ⓐ Across from the Torre Latinoamericana).

LIFESTYLE
Mexican life

LIFESTYLE

Food & drink

Mexican cuisine is one of the most exciting and creative in the world. Reflecting the country's history, it is a blend of the Old and New World. Pre-Colombian influences mean local ingredients like tomatoes, corn and chilli are used, while the use of chicken, beef, onions and garlic is a result of the country's Spanish and French heritage.

Expect to tuck into much more than just tacos and refried beans. You can enjoy a wide variety of fruit and vegetables, great steaks and delicious fish and seafood. In tourist areas international food is easy to find, but vegetarians may have a hard time.

There are more than 100 different types of chilli and not all of them are hot. Mexican dishes are not necessarily spicy and you can always order them *sin chile* (without chilli).

MEAL TIMES

Mexicans eat at any time of the day and food is nearly always on offer from street stalls. Locals will often have two breakfasts. The first, a snack of fruit and bread, is eaten at home, followed by a meal at 10.00 or 11.00 of eggs and tortillas. Lunch,

▶ *Seafood platter*

LIFESTYLE

served from around 13.30, is usually the main meal of the day and can continue for several hours. Snacks are often eaten between 18.00 and 20.00 hours, followed by a light dinner, although restaurants serve big meals in the evening.

TYPES OF RESTAURANT
Most of the large hotels serve buffet evening meals and many have a selection of restaurants serving different cuisines. *Fondas* are good-value, family-run restaurants with fixed lunch menus that are usually

MEXICAN DISHES

Mexicans eat tortillas like we eat bread. These corn pancakes are stuffed, rolled up and toasted or baked to make *enchiladas*, *tostadas*, *tacos* or *quesadillas*. *Frijoles* (beans) are eaten with just about everything and are usually mashed, refried or served whole in stews or soups. *Chiles en nogada* is the national dish, symbolizing Mexican independence and only available between August and October. It is made with Poblano chillies (spicy green peppers) stuffed with meat and covered in a white cream sauce and red pomegranate seeds – the three colours representing the Mexican flag.

Gold tequila is not necessarily of superior quality, and often has colourings, and even flavourings, added. Consult the locals if you want to try the best tequila.

DRINKS

Tequila, distilled from the blue agave plant, is Mexico's national drink and enjoyed all over the world. Drink it straight as a shot, or in a Margarita or Tequila Sunrise cocktail. Mezcal can be made from a number of varieties of agave and often includes a worm as decoration and flavouring. Tequila is never served with a worm. Kahlua is a Mexican, coffee-based liqueur that forms the basis of a Black Russian.

Mexican *cervezas* (beers) are excellent and come in three varieties: light (*clara*), medium (*campechana*) and dark (*oscura*). Corona and Sol are two of the lighter brews; Superior, Bohemia and Dos Equis are somewhat heavier. Mexicans aren't big wine drinkers, but you can find international labels and local wines are usually reasonable. *Jugos* (fresh juices) are a delicious a and healthy option.

▶ *Tequila is Mexico's national drink*

LIFESTYLE

Menu decoder

Common terms and dishes
a la plancha Grilled
al mojo de ajo With garlic sauce
barbacoa Lamb cooked in a pot
caldo largo Soup of fish and seafood
crepa Crepe, usually with a savoury filling
flan Crème caramel
frijoles Beans, often refried
huevos rancheros Fried eggs on fried tortillas with tomato sauce
menú del día Set menu
mole Sauce made with dark chocolate, chillies and spices
pan Bread
pescado a la Veracruzana Red snapper with a tomato, olive and caper sauce
picante Spicy
pollo al pibil Steamed chicken with *achiote*, a local seasoning
postre Dessert
queso Cheese

salsas Sauces usually made with raw vegetables or tomato and chilies.
sopa Soup
tamales Steamed, corn dumplings with meat and chili, wrapped in corn husks or banana leaves
taco Soft or crisp fried tortilla, filled with meat, seafood, beans or cheese
tortilla Omelette
tortillas Thin, round pancakes of corn or wheat
tostada Toast

Meat & seafood
almejas Clams
calamares Squid
camarones Prawns
cangrejo Crab
carne Meat, usually beef
cerdo Pork
chorizo Spicy pork sausage
cordero Lamb
langosta Lobster
mariscos Shellfish
mejillones Mussels
pato Duck
pavo Turkey
pescado Fish
pollo Chicken
pulpo Octopus
tocino Bacon

Fruit & vegetables
coco Coconut
ensalada Salad
fruta Fruit
papa Potato
verduras Vegetables

LIFESTYLE

Shopping

Shopping can be one of the highlights of a Mexican holiday. Everything from traditional handicrafts to contemporary silver jewellery is on offer, whether from the many local markets or designer boutiques.

BARGAINING

Bargaining in Mexico can be viewed as a dance between the two parties – there are very strict moves and it should be enjoyed. Always be polite and good-humoured about the procedure and only start to bargain if you intend to buy the item – breaking off negotiations can be a long process! Decide what you want to pay and ask the seller for the price. Then offer about half of what you want to pay. He or she will more than likely drop the price and then hopefully you can raise your offer to the price you want. If you walk away and they know they are asking too much, they will probably call you back to renegotiate.

ARTS & CRAFTS

Indigenous art and handicrafts are best bought directly from the artisans and workshops that produce them. Reproductions of traditional masks are good buys, as are hand-woven cotton or wool wall hangings and rugs. *Calaveras*, little skeleton figures used as part of the Day of the Dead festival, make great presents, and everywhere you go you will see *muñecas* (hand-made dolls).

Keep an eye out for unusual *nacimientos* (nativity-scene Christmas decorations) made of coloured tin, clay or wood. Semi-precious stones can be found in many shops, with Mexican amber considered the best in the world. Mexico's official handicraft shops, **Fonart**, stock a wonderful variety of handicrafts from all over the country. This organization ploughs back profits into supporting arts and crafts all over the country.

CLOTHING

Guayaberas are traditional shirts worn by Mexican men and boys. Usually white and made of cotton and linen, they are often intricately

LIFESTYLE

embroidered. *Huipiles* are the female versions. A *jorongo* is a wool or cotton rectangular poncho that is a very practical way of staying warm. *Rebozos* are traditional woven shawls, and made of cotton or silk, often featuring beautiful designs.

LEATHER GOODS
Leather shoes and accessories are usually of good quality in Mexico and much cheaper than at home. Look for boots and shoes found in many colours, styles and skins, which can usually be made to measure for a reasonable price. Handbags and wallets are good buys as well.

Handicrafts such as woven baskets and rugs make a good buy

LIFESTYLE

Kids

Mexicans love children and yours will be welcome everywhere that you are. Many of the larger resort hotels have kids clubs, pools and activities for youngsters, and many have babysitting services. On the beach, entertainment comes in the form of swimming, water sports and beach activities. If you venture further afield, there will still be plenty to keep your offspring amused.

If you are travelling with young children, then anywhere from Cancún to Playa del Carmen and all along the Riviera Maya is good to visit. The northern tip of Cancún has the safest beaches because Isla Mujeres blocks the currents there, but there are safe beaches with lifeguards on duty at the other resorts too. The main strip, 5th Avenue, in Playa del Carmen (see page 42) is a great place for older children and teens to shop for clothes and have their hair braided.

ALL THE FUN OF THE FAIR

If you visit the capital, Mexico City, consider taking the kids to **Feria de Chapultepec**. This fun fair has more than 50 rides, including a wooden roller coaster from the 1960s. The day passes are good value.

THEME PARKS

Forty-five minutes from Cancún is **X'Caret Eco Park**, great fun for adults as well as children. On offer is an aquarium, butterfly pavilion, lagoons and a 'Swim with Dolphin Tour'. ❶ 998 883 0470 ⓦ www.xcaret.com

WILDLIFE

Mexico teems with wildlife that will excite most children. In Cozumel (see page 60), Isla Mujeres (see page 27) as well as Puerto Aventuras (see page 51) give them the opportunity to swim with dolphins with **Dolphin Discovery**. ⓦ www.dolphindiscovery.com.mx ❶ Children must be eight years or older

LIFESTYLE

◐ *Making waves on a banana boat*

LIFESTYLE

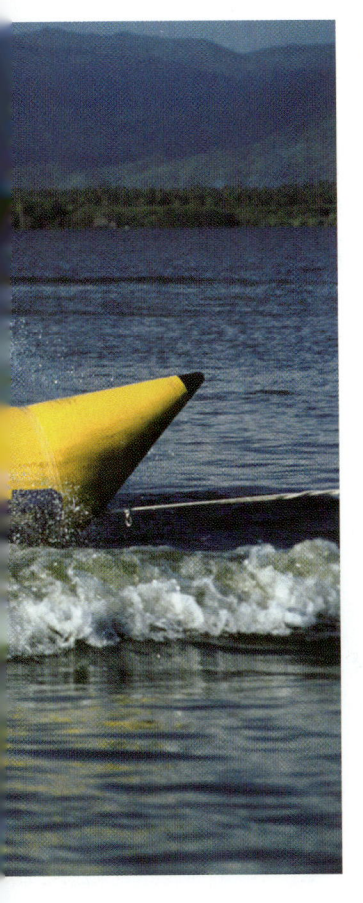

WATER PARKS

Wet 'n Wild in Cancún's Hotel Zone has 244 m (267 yds) of white sand beach and lots of activities for all ages. Parents can relax on the 'Lazy River', and there's also a wave pool, children's playground and 'kamikaze' ride for thrill-seeking teenagers, plus three bars and a large restaurant. Lockers, towels and inner tubs to rent. ⓐ Parque Nizuc, Cancún ⓦ www.wetnwildcancun.com

WATER SPORTS

Most children can't resist the water, whether it is paddling in the sea or taking a boat trip, and there are lots of opportunities for both in this part of Mexico. **Aquaworld** is Cancún's largest water sports centre, offering plenty of options, including a trip on the 'Subsee' explorer, on which kids can explore the coral reef in a glass-bottomed boat. ⓐ Blvd Kukulcán Km 15.2, Zona Hotelera, Cancún ⓣ 998 848 8327 ⓔ info@aquaworld.com.mx ⓦ www.aquaworld.com.mx

105

LIFESTYLE

Sports & activities

The Yucatán, with its miles and miles of coastline and warm climate, offers plenty of opportunities for water sports. The beaches on the Caribbean coast are generally calm and safe, but take heed of local warnings. Most of the popular beaches rent water sports equipment, whether you are looking for a gentle trip around the bay in a pedalo or a thrilling ride on water skis. Opportunities for sailing and boat rides abound, with modern marinas dotted around the coast.

DIVING & SNORKELLING

Mexico has some of the best diving sites in the world and the Yucatán boasts the world's second-largest coral reef, parts of which were made famous by Jacques Cousteau. Calm waters allow for excellent visibility and facilities are mostly of a good standard.

The Caribbean Sea has visibility of 15–45 m (50–150 ft) and wonderfully warm waters that rarely drop below 21°C (70°F). Around Cancún (see page 16), there are a dozen excellent diving sites, many of which are conveniently located near the larger hotels.

The island of Isla Mujeres (see page 27) features dive sites such as the **'Cave of the Sleeping Sharks'**, where close encounters with sharks can be had, and **Garrafón National Marine Park**, with good visitor facilities. The island of Cozumel (see page 60) alone has over 100 dive sites, many of which are shallow enough for snorkelling. Divers can explore plunging walls, underwater caverns, swimming among rare coral, giant sponges and an incredible variety of tropical fish – no less than 250 species. At the **Chankanaab Park** on Cozumel, there is a lagoon that is perfect for beginners.

The Riviera Maya is dotted with good snorkelling sites. These include the resort of Playa del Carmen (see page 42), Xcaret '**Eco-Park**' (see page 82), Akumal and the reserve of **Xel-Ha** (see page 85) with its fresh springs. Further south again is the World Heritage Site of **Sian Ka'an Biosphere**

◗ *Tropical fish are a sight to see in the clear Yucatán waters*

LIFESTYLE

Reserve (see page 82) and a 96 km (60 mile) chain of coral reefs. *Cenote* and cave diving are both very popular, but only for the experienced.

FISHING
Some of the best deep-sea fishing in the world is found off the Caribbean coast. Tuna, sea bass and swordfish are all common catches. All of the resorts featured in this book are home to operators who can arrange fishing trips, for just a few hours, or for a few weeks.

GOLF
Mexico is a fast-growing golf destination, partly thanks to its beautiful, diverse scenery, and Cancún is now one of the country's top golfing destinations. Cancún's 18-hole courses include the pretty, lagoon-side **Pok-Ta-Pok Golf Course** (a Blvd Kukulcán Km 7.5, Zona Hotelera ❶ 998 883 1230 ⓦ http://www.cancungolfclub.com/) and the **Hilton Cancún Beach & Golf Resort** (see page 19).

LIFESTYLE

Festivals & events

Many of Mexico's celebrations are regional affairs and are often based around a religious event; many celebrate local patron saints. You will find small fairs and harvest festivals taking place year-round, but there are also several big, national events. There's Carnaval, of course – the third largest in the world after Rio and New Orleans – as well as Easter (which constitutes the Holy Week, or Semana Santa), The Day of the Dead, Independence Day, the Day of the Virgin of Guadalupe and Christmas, which are all celebrated throughout the country with wholehearted festivity.

THE DAY OF THE DEAD

A more unusual celebration in Mexico is The Day of the Dead (*El Dia de los Muertos*), which takes place on 2 November, also known as All Soul's Day (the lead up to this is All Saint's Day, on 1 November). This is not a macabre event, but is when Mexicans remember their dead loved ones, bringing presents of food, candles and incense to their graveside in the belief that their spirits might return on this day. Skulls and skeletons made out of sugar, papier-mâché and other materials can be seen in the shops and special bread is made.

THE FEAST OF THE VIRGIN OF GUADALUPE

This huge, nationwide event – and one of Mexico's most important expressions of traditional culture – is held to honour Mexico's patron saint, said to have appeared to a young man called Juan Diego in 1531 on a hill near Mexico City. A traditional 'Happy Birthday' song is sung at dawn and there are special church services, followed by dancing and fireworks. Celebrations start on 1 December and carry through to 12 December, with local variations, depending on where you are.

Check the date of celebrations, particularly Easter and Carnaval, as they may vary by a few days from year to year.

LIFESTYLE

CALENDAR OF EVENTS

January

6 January	**Three Kings Day** commemorates the Three Kings bringing gifts to Jesus. Children are given presents and a special cake is eaten.

February

2 February	**Candlemas** marks the end of winter with parties at homes and in the street.
5 February	Street festivities on **Constitution Day** celebrate the signing of the Mexican constitution in 1917.
Week before Lent	**Carnaval** is an exuberant, five-day festival, which sometimes falls in March.

March

21 March	**Benito Juárez's Birthday** is a national holiday in honour of the impoverished Zapotec Indian who became one of Mexico's most loved presidents.

April

Palm Sun–Easter Sun	**Holy Week,** which includes Easter, with religious processions. The country's biggest holiday period.

May

1 May	**Labour Day** is a national holiday.
5 May	**Cinco de Mayo** commemorates the Battle of Puebla of 1862 when the Mexicans successfully fought off the invading French army.

June

1 June	**Navy Day** is honoured in coastal towns by naval parades and fireworks.
29 June	**St. Peter and St. Paul's Day** is observed in various locations.

LIFESTYLE

Day of the Dead figurines are a treasured part of Mexican culture

LIFESTYLE

LIFESTYLE

August

13 August — **Fall of Tenochtitlán** commemorates the last battle of the Spanish Conquest and the surrender of the last Aztec king to Cortez. The loss of thousands of lives are remembered in wreath-laying ceremonies in Mexico City.

15 August — **Feast of the Assumption** – religious processions.

September

15–16 September — **Independence Day** is an important national holiday that celebrates Mexico's independence from Spain with parades and family parties.

October

12 October — **El Día de la Raza**, originally celebrated Columbus arriving in the Americas, but now honours the ancient Mexicans.

November

1–2 November — **The Day of the Dead** is a national holiday that continues for two days and includes All Saint's Day and All Soul's Day (see page 108).

20 November — **Revolution Day** is a national holiday that commemorates the start of the Mexican Revolution in 1910. The day is filled with parades, speeches, rodeos, and patriotic events.

December

12 December — **The Feast of the Virgin of Guadalupe.**

16–24 December — **Posadas** celebrates Mary and Joseph's search for a lodging, with re-enacted door-to-door candlelight processions.

25 December — **Christmas** is celebrated with a church service.

PRACTICAL INFORMATION
Tips & advice

PRACTICAL INFORMATION

Preparing to go

GETTING THERE

There are plenty of tour operators offering package holidays to the Yucatán. Most people pop into their local travel agent and start flicking through brochures of the popular resorts, and this is often the best way to find a package you like. Travel agents often have insider knowledge about certain hotels, and this can be very useful. An exhaustive list of tour operators is given on the UK version of the Mexican Tourist Board's website (W www.mexicotravel.co.uk). If you are looking for something out of the ordinary, perhaps a longer and more varied itinerary than usual, then it's a good idea to speak to a specialist travel agent. **Journey Latin America** (T 020 8747 8315 W www.journeylatinamerica.co.uk) and **Trailfinders** (T 020 7938 3939 W www.trailfinders.com) are highly rated.

By air

If you want to get there with a scheduled airline consider flying via the capital. British Airways (T 0870 850 9850 W www.ba.com) fly non-stop from Heathrow to Mexico City, and the journey takes around 12 hours. Other carriers operating direct flights to Mexico City from Europe (but not London) include Air France (T 0870 142 4343 W www.airfrance.com), Lufthansa (T 0845 7737 747 W www.lufthansa.co.uk) and Spain's

> **PREVENTING JETLAG**
>
> You may think jet lag is a myth, but don't underestimate the effects of being in the air for more than ten hours. The atmosphere in a cabin is drier than the Sahara desert and your body can quickly begin to dehydrate. Drink plenty of water, both before boarding the plane and whilst flying. Experienced flyers refuse any kind of alcohol on board and carry their own bottles of water, as the amount the crew offer isn't enough. Be sure to move around the aircraft during the flight to prevent circulation problems.

national carrier, Iberia (☎ 0845 601 2854 ⓦ www.iberia.com). An alternative is to fly with one of the US airlines, and this usually involves a stop or change in somewhere like Miami. However, getting through US customs can be a real chore, so think long and hard before choosing this option.

BEFORE YOU LEAVE

No particular inoculations are recommended for Mexico, but check with the Department of Health (ⓦ www.dh.gov.uk) or the World Health Organization (ⓦ www.who.int/en) for the latest information. It is always a good idea to be up to date on your tetanus, typhoid and polio immunisations, however. Malaria and dengue fever can be a problem, but this is only in certain rural regions that very few tourists are likely to visit.

If you are taking prescription medicines, ensure that you take enough for the duration of your visit, and an extra copy of the information sheet in case of loss. Note that you may find it impossible to obtain the same medicines in Mexico, however. It is also worth having a dental check-up before you leave the UK.

A small first-aid kit can bring peace of mind, especially if you have small children. Consider including painkillers, plasters, antiseptic cream, travel sickness tablets and a remedy for upset stomachs. Repellent and light, long-sleeved clothing can give protection from mosquitoes. It is a good idea to bring sun tan lotion with you, because the factor number system is not always as reliable in Mexico as it is in the UK. Bear in mind that if you are not fussy about brands most toiletries are considerably cheaper than in the UK. Brands such as 'Tampax' and 'Wet Ones' are often hard to find. Nappies and moisturising creams are available, but you might want to bring some with you. The often-intense heat should not be underestimated: use plenty of sunscreen, wear a hat and take cover in the heat of the day.

DOCUMENTS

The most important documents you will need are your tickets and your passport. Check well in advance that your passport is up to date and has at least three months left to run (six months is even better). All children,

PRACTICAL INFORMATION

including newborn babies, need their own passport now. It generally takes at least three weeks to process a passport renewal. This can be longer in the run-up to the summer months. Contact the **Passport Agency** for the latest information on how to renew your passport and the processing times involved (☎ 0870 521 0410 🌐 www.ukpa.gov.uk).

As police do occasionally ask foreigners for ID, it is a good idea to take a photocopy of your passport to keep with you when you are out and about. Make sure the details of your plane tickets are correct well in advance. If you do think you might want to drive, bring your driving licence, along with the licence of anybody else who intends to drive. By law, you must always carry your licence while driving in Mexico.

MONEY

You will need some currency before you go, especially if your flight gets you to your destination at the weekend or late in the day after the banks have closed. You can exchange money at the airport before you depart.

Once you arrive, you will find cash dispensers in all the resorts. Just look for the round blue 'Cirrus' sign to use your switch card, or for the 'Mastercard' or 'Visa' logo to withdraw money from a credit card account. However, if you are planning to visit a quiet beach or a small mountain village, make sure you have enough cash to at least buy something to eat, and to get a taxi back to your hotel in an emergency.

You should also make sure that your credit, charge and debit cards are up to date – you do not want them to expire mid-holiday – and that your credit limit is sufficient to allow you to make those holiday purchases. Do not forget, too, to check your PIN numbers in case you have not used them for a while – ring your bank or card company and they will help you out. Also make a note of your bank's 24-hour emergency line to call.

TELEPHONING MEXICO
To call Mexico from the UK, dial 00 52 then the city or area code followed by the seven- or eight-digit local number.

PRACTICAL INFORMATION

INSURANCE
Annual insurance policies can make economical sense, depending on how often you go abroad. Shop around and check the small print and ensure you are covered for any extra activities such as scuba diving, horse riding, or water sports – and for emergency medical and dental treatment, including flights home if required, and especially if you suffer from any chronic health conditions.

CLIMATE
The Yucatán's beach resorts are usually hot and humid the whole year round, but from June to August, temperatures can be unbearable. There is a chance of rain throughout the year, and the hurricane season runs from June to November. Sites such as Ⓦ www.weather.com can provide the latest weather information.

SECURITY
Take sensible precautions while you are away:
- Cancel milk, newspapers and other regular deliveries.
- Let the postman know where to leave bulky mail.
- If possible, arrange for someone to visit regularly, closing and opening your curtains, and switching lights on and off. Or buy electrical timing devices that will switch lights and radios on and off.
- Let Neighbourhood Watch representatives know that you will be away so that they can keep an eye on your home.
- If you have a burglar alarm, make sure that it is working properly and is switched on when you leave.
- If you are leaving cars unattended, put them in a garage, if possible, and leave a key with a neighbour in case the alarm goes off.

CHECK-IN, PASSPORT CONTROL & CUSTOMS
Airport security can be intimidating, but it is all very easy, really.
- Check-in desks usually open two or three hours before the flight is due to depart. Arrive early for the best choice of seats.

PRACTICAL INFORMATION

- Look for your flight number on the TV monitors in the check-in area, and find the relevant check-in desk. Your tickets will be checked and your luggage taken. Take your boarding card and go to the departure gate. Here your hand luggage will be X-rayed and your passport checked.
- In the departure area, the monitors tell you when to board – usually about 30 minutes before take-off. Go to the departure gate shown and follow the instructions given to you by the airline staff.

Pack nail scissors and/or penknives in your checked-in luggage, rather than in hand luggage – these are not allowed in the cabin.

During your stay

ARRIVAL
Formata Migratoria de Turista card
Tourists venturing more than 30 km (19 miles) past the Mexican border will need a *Forma Migratoria de Turista* (FMT), a free form available at borders, airports, ports and Mexican embassies and tourist offices. You must show a passport valid for six months from the date of travel, proof of finances and proof of a return or onward ticket. The form is valid for 180 days and it must be carried on your person at all times.

BEACHES
All Mexican beaches are public property, although in practice it is often difficult to access a beach without walking through a hotel's property.

CHILDREN'S ACTIVITIES
Babysitters can usually be arranged at larger hotels, many of which provide day activities for children. See page 103 for further options.

CONSULATES & EMBASSIES
If you are unlucky enough to need the help of the British Government, you will need to contact the Consular Section of the British Embassy in

PRACTICAL INFORMATION

Mexico City or an Honorary Consulate (Cancún is the only office in the Yucatán). A full list of Embassy offices is available at their website (w www.britishembassy.gov.uk/mexico) and details of the Cancún and Mexico City offices are give below:
Cancún ❸ Honorary Consulate, Royal Sands, Blvd Kukulkan Km 13.5, Zona Hotelera, 77500 Cancún ❶ 998 881 0100
Mexico City ❸ British Embassy Consular Section, Río Usumacinta 26, Col Cuauhtémoc, 06500 México DF ❶ 55 5242 8500

CURRENCY

The peso is the Mexican monetary unit, but US dollars are widely accepted. The peso comes in denominations of 10, 20 and 50 centavos (cents) and 1, 2, 5, 10 and 20 pesos; bills come in denominations of 20, 50, 100, 200, 500 pesos. The symbol, $, is similar to the US dollar, so you will often find 'MN' placed after it, for *moneda nacional* (national currency).

ELECTRICITY

Mexico's electricity system is 120 V/60 Hz, usually using two flat-pin plugs, so bring a socket adaptor if you plan to use electrical equipment from home. Anything you bring with you that operates at a higher rate of 240V (such as a hairdryer) will need to be dual-voltage. Those that

BEACH SAFETY

Take heed of local warnings about currents, which can be dangerous, and be aware that water sports equipment may not meet British safety standards. On the ocean side, coloured flags indicate the safety of the surf. Note that they are different from those in Europe. Green or Blue Flags mean the water is calm and safe for swimming. Yellow Flags indicate that swimmers should exercise caution. Red or Black Flags denote dangerous conditions such as strong undertow; swimmers should get out of the water until lifeguards signal an improvement in the sea's condition.

PRACTICAL INFORMATION

operate on 12 volts with the use of a special adaptor (transformer) will usually cope with dual voltage, but check before travel.

FACILITIES FOR VISITORS WITH DISABILITIES
Visitors with disabilities may find travel around Mexico difficult. There are few wheelchair ramps, and escalators are far more common than lifts. Visits to the country's world-famous archaeological sites may prove particularly trying. That said, if you choose to stay in one location and pick your accommodation carefully, you are likely to find fewer problems. Newer and more expensive hotels and private villas may have excellent adaptations. Cancún has one of the better-equipped airports in the country, with ramps, disabled toilets and wheelchairs available on request. Ask your travel agent for details, or contact a specialist operator.

GETTING AROUND
Driving
Car hire Major international car rental companies have offices in most cities, airports and bus stations, although local companies are cheaper. Pre-booking is ideal, but be sure that the price includes 15 per cent tax and full insurance (with theft and collision damage waiver). Drivers must have a driver's licence, be over 21 (or 25) and have a major credit card.
Rules of the road Distances are measured in kilometres, and driving is on the right-hand side of the road. Seat belts are compulsory and speed limits are: 40 kph (25 mph) in cities; 70 kph (45 mph) in rural areas; and 110 kph (68 mph) on motorways.
Roads Most Mexican road surfaces are uneven, with plenty of potholes and traffic. Speedbumps can often be very high, and unmarked. If you are in need of breakdown assistance, the Ángeles Verdes – English-speaking mechanics who patrol the major highways in bright green trucks – offer a free service, except for spare parts, fuel and a discretionary tip, provided by Mexico's Ministry of Trouism (SECTUR). There are toll roads (*cuota*), free roads (*libre*), and *super carreteras*, expensive but fast motorways. Drivers are insured against accident or breakdown on *cuotas*.

PRACTICAL INFORMATION

Petrol Almost every town will have a Government-controlled Pemex station. All petrol is unleaded and is priced by the litre.
Parking A white E (*estacionamiento*) on a blue background indicates a parking lot. A black E in a red circle means parking is permitted. The same E with a diagonal line through it means no parking.

Public transport
Buses Intercity and long-distance buses can vary dramatically in quality and cost – it is best to go for the more luxurious option. Local buses, or *camiones*, are cheap but have pre-set stops. Minibuses, or *colectivos*, are cheaper than taxis and a step up from the crowded buses. Wave one down and tell the driver where you want to go. The fare is established by the government, depending on how far you go. Pay at the end of the journey.
Taxis Taxis are common and can be economical if you have luggage. Establish if the driver has a meter – if not, confirm a price first.
Ferries These go to Isla Cozumel from Puerto Morelos (car ferry) and Playa del Carmen (passenger only). Ferries also run from Puerto Juárez (passenger only) and Punta Sam (car ferry) to Isla Mujeres. Another ferry leaves for Isla Mujeres from Cancún's Playa Linda several times daily.

HEALTH MATTERS
Chemists Major resorts will have several *farmácias*. Oral rehydration tablets are free of charge at health centres if suffering from diarrhoea.
Health hazards Beware of jellyfish and coral while swimming – if cut or bitten, be sure to bathe and disinfect. Avoid sunstroke when on a long walk or tour – carry oral rehydration salts, sunscreen, hats and bottled water. If visiting high-altitude areas, allow time to acclimatize – tiredness, shortness of breath and headaches are symptoms of altitude sickness.
Water Only drink bottled water, as tap water can often result in an upset stomach. Also, avoid ice in cold drinks and be wary of street food stalls.
Clinics Visitors must rely on either private treatment or go to the local Civil Hospital (*Centro de Salud*) or Red Cross hospital. Check with your hotel, embassy or tourist office for a list of English-speaking doctors.

PRACTICAL INFORMATION

THE LANGUAGE

Mexicans love it if you try to speak even a little Spanish, and are also very patient. Below are a few basic words and phrases to get you started.

ENGLISH	SPANISH (pronunciation)
General vocabulary	
yes	*si*
no	*no*
please	*por favor*
thank you (very much)	*(muchas) gracias*
you're welcome	*de nada*
hello	*hola*
goodbye	*adios*
good morning/day	*buenas dias*
good afternoon/evening	*buenas tardes*
good evening (after dark)	*buenas noches*
excuse me (to get attention)	*disculpe*
excuse me (to apologise)	*perdóneme*
sorry	*lo siento*
help!	*socorro!*
today	*hoy*
tomorrow	*manana*
yesterday	*ayer*
Useful words & phrases	
How much is it?	*Quanto es?*
Expensive	*Caro/a*
I don't understand	*No entiendo*
Do you speak English?	*Hablas Inglés?*
My name is...	*Me llamo...*

OPENING HOURS

Shops are usually open between 09.00 and 19.00 or 20.00 hours, and closed for lunch between 14.00 and 16.00. Most shops close on Sundays,

PRACTICAL INFORMATION

although large shopping centres may stay open, particularly in tourist areas and Mexico City. Banks are usually open Mon–Fri 09.00–13.30 and museums are open Tues–Sun 09.00–17.00 and archaeological sites are open Mon–Fri 08.00–17.00. Churches are in frequent use, so be aware of potentially disturbing a service.

PERSONAL COMFORT & SAFETY

Crime prevention Although most tourist areas in the Yucatán are relatively safe, it makes sense not to wear expensive jewellery and flaunt valuable electrical goods. Pick-pocketing in crowded areas does occur. Avoid withdrawing large sums of money from cash points and try not to take out money or drive late at night.

Lost property If you have anything lost or stolen, you should report it to the local police and obtain a statement in order to claim on your insurance at home. Lost passports should be reported to your embassy.

Police There are several different types of police in Mexico, from traffic and tourist police, to police hired to work on contract to banks and businesses. As a general rule, the police are best avoided, but the federal trafffic police will help those stuck on the highway, and the tourist police can often speak some English.

POST OFFICES

Most resorts will have an *oficina de correos* for stamps and to send or receive post. Rates change often, so check first. For airmail, mark it 'Por Avión' – remember it can take up to three weeks to reach Europe.

TELEPHONES

For long-distance calls within the country, dial 01 plus the area code then the number. For example, the area code for Cancún is 998. From outside Cancun, you will need to dial 01, then the three-digit code, followed by the seven-digit number. From within Cancun, however, omit the codes and dial only the seven-digit number.

To phone the UK, dial 00 44, followed by the area code (minus the 0) and the number.

PRACTICAL INFORMATION

> **EMERGENCY NUMBERS**
> Ambulance 065
> Police 060

TIME DIFFERENCES
The Yucatán is five hours behind GMT, although much of the rest of the Mexico is on Central Standard Time which is six hours behind GMT.

TIPPING
Service in smarter restaurants is sometimes included in the bill, but if not, add on 10 to 15 per cent – preferably in cash. Taxi drivers do not expect tips, but you can round up the fare. Tipping of tour leaders is at your discretion. Hotel room cleaners will always value a tip.

TOURIST INFORMATION OFFICES
The UK Mexican Tourist Office's website has some basic information and travel hints. 020 7488 9392 www.mexicotravel.co.uk

Local tourist offices
Cancún Avenida Tulum 26 998 884 8073
Cozumel Corner of Avenida Benito Juarez and Avenida 5 987 872 0972
Isla Mujeres Avenida Rueda Medina between Morelos and Madero 998 877 0767
Mérida There is a small information booth at the airport. The main office in the centre of the city is at the Palacio de Gobierno (Government Palace) just off the Plaza Grande (Main Square) 999 924 9290
Mexico City Amberes No.54, esq. Londres, Col. Juarez 55 533 4700
Playa del Carmen Avenida Tulum 26 984 884 8073

… INDEX

INDEX

A
air tours 88–90
Akumal 14, 66–72, 106
ancient sites *see* Chichén Itzá; Cobá; Mayan sites; Teotihuacán; Tulum
aquarium 14, 61, 94, 103
aviary 44
Aztecs 78, 91

B
beaches 13, 14, 20–1, 22, 27, 28–9, 39, 44, 47, 53, 62, 70, 103, 105, 106, 118, 119
bike rides 66, 85
bird watching 14, 21, 30, 38, 44, 69, 82, 89
boat trips 13, 30, 47, 53, 61, 62, 71
  glass-bottomed boats 13, 61, 105
  sunset cruise 13, 61

C
Cancún 9, 13, 14, 16–26, 55, 70, 90, 105, 106, 107
Carnaval 108, 109
Catedral Metropolitana 14, 92
Cathedral of San Idelfonso 86, 87
CEDAM Shipwreck Museum 51
Chankanaab Park 14, 61, 106
Chichén Itzá 14, 21, 30, 75–6, 90
children 20, 47, 61, 62, 66, 70, 103–5, 118
Cobá 14, 77–8, 79
convent 12, 14, 86
coral reefs 17, 36, 39, 43, 47, 55, 60, 61, 70, 105, 107
Cousteau, Jacques 60, 106
Cozumel 13, 14, 19, 47, 48, 55, 60–5, 70, 89, 103
crafts 26, 35, 41, 64, 72, 92, 101
crocodiles 36, 62

D
Day of the Dead 11, 101, 108, 112
diving 14, 19, 20, 21, 38, 43, 51, 53, 55, 60, 61, 70, 106
  cave diving 38, 43, 107
  night diving 70
  scuba diving 14
  shallow cave diving (*cenote*) 70, 107
  tank diving 38
  wall diving 38, 55
dolphins 82, 89
  bottlenose dolphins 13, 19, 48
  swimming with 19, 27, 48, 56, 61, 103

E
El Garrfón Eco Park 27, 29
El Rey 19
excursions 21–2, 30, 39, 47–8, 55–6, 62, 70–1, 73–94

F
festivals and events 10–11, 108–9, 112
fishing 14, 17, 55, 61, 71
  bone fishing 61
  bottom fishing 55
  deep-sea fishing 48, 61, 107
  sport fishing 39, 48, 66–7
food and drink 96–100
football 38
fun fair 103

G
golf 14, 19, 43–4, 51, 53, 61, 71, 107

H
Hacienda Mundaca 29
Holbox Island 89
horse riding 38, 56

I
Isla Contoy 30
Isla Mujeres 13, 19, 20, 27–35, 89, 90, 103, 106
Isla Pajaros 89

J
jet-skis 20
jungle trips 13, 39, 44, 56, 66

126

INDEX

K / L
kayaks 20, 29
language 9, 10, 99–100, 122

M
marinas 48, 51, 53, 54, 71, 106
marine life 13, 27, 47, 69, 89, 106
  conservation areas 14
  crocodile zoo 36
  parks 14, 19, 48, 61, 82, 85, 106
  see also dolphins; turtles
markets 17, 26, 65, 72, 92
Mayan sites 9, 14, 19, 21, 30, 39, 43, 44, 75–8, 80
  see also Chichén Itzá; Cobá; Tulum
menu decoder 99–100
Mérida 14, 29, 86, 87, 90
Mexico City 14, 78, 91–4, 103

N
natural wells 13, 39, 44, 56, 86
nature parks and reserves 14, 21, 36, 38, 61–2, 82
  marine parks 14, 19, 48, 61, 82, 85, 106
  Sian Ka'an Biosphere 14, 21, 30, 82, 106–7

P
parasailing 20, 53, 62
Playa del Carmen & Playacar 13, 36, 42–50, 56, 62, 89, 103, 106
Puerto Aventuras 13, 48, 51–9, 71, 103
Puerto Morelos 13, 36–41

Q
quad-biking 13, 38, 44

S
San Miguel 60
Sea Trek 29
seals 13
shopping 26, 35, 41, 50, 58, 65, 72, 92, 101–2
markets 17, 26, 65, 72, 92
opening hours 26, 122–3
Sian Ka'an Biosphere 14, 21, 30, 82, 106–7
snorkelling 13, 14, 19, 20, 21, 22, 27, 29, 35, 36, 39, 47, 53, 55, 56, 60, 61, 62, 69, 70, 71, 82, 85, 106–7
snuba 27–8, 61
submarine trip 61
surfing 13
swimming 13, 20, 27, 30, 55, 60, 62, 69, 71, 82, 85
  with dolphins 19, 27, 48, 56, 61, 103
  in natural wells 13, 44, 56, 86

T
tennis 53, 71
Teotihuacán 14, 78, 80
theme parks 103
tube rides 20
Tulum 14, 20, 22, 30, 56, 62, 80, 85
turtles 13, 30, 38, 47, 53
  turtle sanctuary 29
  turtle walk 68–9

V
Valladolid 12, 14, 86
Virgin of Guadalupe 10–11, 108, 112
visitors with disabilities 120
volleyball 20

W
water parks 19, 105
water sports 13, 38, 53, 62, 70, 105, 106
wildlife 14, 21, 36, 38, 44, 56, 82, 85, 89, 103
  see also marine life

X
Xcaret 14, 82, 85, 103, 106
Xel-Ha 14, 22, 84, 85, 106

Y / Z
Yal Kú Lagoon 69
zoos 29, 36

ACKNOWLEDGEMENTS

We would like to thank all the photographers, picture libraries and organisations for the loan of the photographs reproduced in this book, to whom copyright in the photograph belongs:
Jane Egginton (pages 5, 8, 10, 15, 18, 24, 34, 73, 74, 76, 81, 90, 93, 97, 102, 104); Jesus Javier Fernandez Vinuesa/Alamy (page 41); JupiterImages Corporation (pages 83, 107, 113, 125); Macduff Everton/Corbis (page 84); Lawson Wood/Corbis (page 88); Nik Wheeler/Corbis (page 31); PCL/Alamy (page 32); Sue Clark/Alamy (page 68); Copyright Thomas Cook (pages 1, 12, 20, 45, 46, 54, 57, 79, 87, 95, 99).

We would also like to thank the following for their contribution to this series:
John Woodcock (map and symbols artwork);
Katie Greenwood (picture research);
Patricia Baker, Rachel Carter, Judith Chamberlain-Webber, Nicky Falkof, Nicky Gyopari, Robin Pridy (editorial support);
Christine Engert, Suzie Johanson, Richard Lloyd, Richard Peters, Alistair Plumb, Jane Prior, Barbara Theisen, Ginny Zeal, Barbara Zuñiga (design support).

Send your thoughts to
books@thomascook.com

- **Found a beach bar, peaceful stretch of sand or must-see sight that we don't feature?**
- **Like to tip us off about any information that needs a little updating?**
- **Want to tell us what you love about this handy, little guidebook and more importantly how we can make it even handier?**

Then here's your chance to tell all! Send us ideas, discoveries and recommendations today and then look out for your valuable input in the next edition of this title. And, as an extra 'thank you' from Thomas Cook Publishing, you'll be automatically entered into our exciting monthly prize draw.

Send an email to the above address or write to:
HotSpots Project Editor, Thomas Cook Publishing, PO Box 227, Unit 15/16, Coningsby Road, Peterborough PE3 8SB, UK.